Busy Moments of an Idle Woman

Susan Petigru King
with a new foreword
by Angela Hanyak

Soigné Books
Charleston, SC

Published in the United States by Soigné Books, Charleston, SC.

www.soignebooks.com

Soigné Books are available at special discounts for bulk purchases for educational or organizational use. For more information, email hello@soignebooks.com.

Library of Congress Cataloging-in-Publication Data is available upon request.

ISBN 978-0-6924-9455-4

First published in 1853 by D. Appleton & Company

PRINTED IN THE UNITED STATES OF AMERICA

Foreword by Angela Hanyak

10 9 8 7 6 5 4 3 2 1

Second Edition

"To my sister, who the first commended these trifles, I dedicate them; and I call upon her to bear with me the fate whom (if noticed at all) may befall them; for though to our owlish eyes these fledglings seem "very pretty birds indeed," yet to the eagle glances of critics, and to indifferent readers, they will probably appear stupid good-for-noughts, only fit to be disposed of at one fell swoop.

June, 1853."

Contents

FOREWORD

Susan Petigru King expected to be forgotten by the ages. In dedicating her first novel to her sister, she wonders if the stories will be "noticed at all." While the history books remember her friend Mary Boykin Chestnut and her diary of the Civil War, King's stories of high society ladies, fast men and water-place life are largely disregarded. And this is a downright shame.

King crafted stories that were driven by strong, determined women hellbent on finding their own happiness in a time when such women were regarded as scandalous. From the self-sufficient

Edith Woodville to the sweetly vengeful Rosa Sydney, King's characters are focused on advancing their own interests rather than playing a supporting role in the lives of the men around them.

In our modern age of online dating and "swiping right," King's stories are a refreshing reminder that smart women need not settle. Paradoxically, King regards marriage as a black box of quick-changing temperaments and uncertain happiness while idolizing true, romantic love, free of marital pressure, as the ultimate prize to be won. Her heroines do not marry for money, status or security; rather, they are only moved into the institution by independent love. Those women who have conformed to marriage are exposed to young widowhood, abusive husbands and extramarital flirtations.

But King avoids denigrating her male characters; they are by equal measure forced into unhappy marriages and made victims of female coquetry. She instead seems to envy them. They are beautiful and carefree, like Charley Staunton's band of cigar-smoking dandies, and prone to rakish antics, as with Harry Newton's social commentary.

The two main sources of malevolence in King's stories are elders and gossips, fitting allegories for the the societal expectations of the time and the consequences of failing to comply with their norms. Mrs. Mourdant's arch nemesis, Miss Weston, is the embodiment of both elements, an old maid and fervent gossip who "must always find something new" to tattle about.

Reading King's stories from a twenty-first century perspective imbues the reader with an appreciation for the social freedoms widely enjoyed by women today. But her depictions of feminine discontent, a form of realism rarely found in Antebellum literature, have been overlooked in favor of historical and political works from the era. Perhaps a fresh discovery of King's works will give readers a fuller understanding of the history of American womanhood and her various dispositions in the years prior to the War Between the States.

EDITH

CHAPTER I.

"Close the window, Edith. The light shines in my eyes," complained the sick man in a languid tone.

"Yes, dear father—let me just add the last tint to this distant tree, and then I am at your commands." As she spoke, a girl rose from the table at which she was drawing, and after closing the shutter, advanced to the other side of the room, where the invalid, partly propped up by pillows, reclined upon a couch. "Do you feel better, papa?" she asked, gently taking his worn and thin hand within her own.

"I am freer from pain than I have been for several days. But Edith, love, I do not like you to remain so long bending over your work. Come, it is some time since I have heard one of your songs."

"A song, papa, without accompaniment! Then I must fancy myself a poet of old and 'sing to the myrtle!'" With assumed gayety she separated a sprig from a bouquet on the table, and in a low, soft, yet evidently powerful voice, began an old-fashioned, very sweet ballad.

"Thank you, dear," said the invalid, sighing deeply when she had finished. He drew his daughter nearer to him, and pressed his pale lips to her brow. Conquering a momentary weakness, she raised her head, and brushing a glistening tear from her eye.

"Will you have a hymn now, papa?" she asked. "I have just learnt such a glorious one—listen!" and she commenced "The spacious firmament on high."

The father listened entranced, his very breath seemed suspended. Unconsciously his head sank upon the pillow; his eyes closed, he slept. Gently warbling the last lingering notes, Edith bent over the slumberer, noiselessly arranged the covering, and then with light step returned to her work. An hour passed, and still her father stirred not. The brush was without ceasing rapidly plied, and she was beginning to rejoice at his quiet and lengthened repose, when the sick man's voice called her again to his side.

"Support my head, dearest, I am fainting." The terrified girl had presence of mind enough to ring the bell, and then resting her father's head against her bosom, she gazed with intense interest upon those loved features now fast stiffening in death. "My time has at length arrived, my darling, and thanks to that God who reigns above eternal, I do not think I regret to leave this world. He who provides for 'the fatherless' will surely not forsake you. Pray to him, dear daughter. Remember you mother—be like her. I go to join her. Ellen, I shall —"

His voice grew faint and his respiration was difficult. He grasped his daughter's hand more tightly. The nurse, who had hastened to the room at the sound of the bell, perceiving at a glance how matters stood, relieved Edith from her charge. The girl threw herself on her knees beside her father. She bedewed his hands with her tears. She entreated him to bless her, to speak her name once more. The eyelids of the dying man slightly quivered, and in broken accents he continued:

"In my desk, yonder, Edith, you will find a small packet directed to yourself. After my death, take it, read it. I can say no more. Farewell, dearest daughter! God forever bless you, my good child! Heavenly Father, receive my spirit!"

A slight noise in his throat proclaimed that the mighty hour had come. A moment more, and the convulsion passed from his face. A calm, angelic smile dwelt there. He again pressed his daughter's hand and expired. With one long wild shriek the orphan cast herself upon the corpse. In vain the nurse attempted to raise her, till at length a burst of tears relieved the overcharged heart. Merely motioning to the woman to make the necessary preparations, she sought her own small chamber, and during many hours wept without ceasing.

The full terrors of her situations, however, seemed to endow her with new force. Knowing and feeling that there was not one creature on whom she could depend, in all that great city, she desired as much as possible to forget the full extent of her loss, and to nerve herself for the trials yet to come. Such was the strength of her character that before the evening closed in, she had been able with tolerable composure to decide upon the time and place for the funeral. The next day, in the humblest manner, but with decency and reverent piety, the father was buried. Edith followed him to his grave. Her landlady insisted upon going with her. She was so sorry, that stirring Yankee woman, for the quiet, regularly paying and respectable young girl, who took no airs upon herself, though she (Mrs. Twiggs) "was sure that they came of high people."

"And have you no friends, miss?" asked Mrs. Twiggs, the next day, when Edith called her to pay the week' rent, and to inform her that she would continue to keep her own room in the house. "But —" and the poor child's voice strove to be calm, "but my father's room I shall no longer need."

"Have you no one, miss, that could take you into the country for a bit? Just to smell the green grass, and sniff up a little fresh air?"

"No, I have no friends, no relations," said Edith bitterly. "I am alone in the world, but don't be afraid for me. I can work just the same, and pay my rent, though my—he is not here. Forgive me," she hastily went on, as even through her fast-filling eyes she saw the mortification her words have given her really kindly-disposed hostess, "forgive me. I see I judged you wrongly, but I feel very suspicious, very hard." and she held out her hand. It was a little, soft, white, delicate hand, with rosy nails, and looks so incapable of work. Mrs. Twiggs was disarmed.

"Poor thing," she said, "poor little thing!" and with surprising tact, she merely pressed the hand,

and left the room.

Edith gave no moments to blinding tears. She began to look over, to remove, and to examine her father's effects. His wardrobe was neither extensive nor rich. Edith packed up the whole in one box. The few books which lay scattered about she carried into her chamber, and then came her greatest effort, to unlock her father's private desk, and to search for the letter, which his dying lips had told her contained his last directions. She found the packet in a secret drawer, and drawing her chair to the table, began to read, as if it were her dead father's voice that addressed her. While thus employed we will go back a few years, and speak of this same father, and of his life.

CHAPTER II.

Albert Millwood was the second and younger son of a very rich, and very influential family. His father, Richard Millwood, of Millwood, was the proudest and most prejudiced of men. Proud of his birth (they could show very far back for Americans), proud of his standing in society, proud of his position in the country, proud of his money, and proudest of all of his two sons. Having himself made an excellent marriage, he naturally expected them to do the same.

John, the elder, dutifully fulfilled the wishes of his parents by wedding Miss Mary Etheredge, a lady in no way remarkable either for her wit or for her beauty, but as she was of a good Southern family, and brought an uncommonly large dowry, Mr. Millwood was perfectly charmed with his daughter-in-law. It had been long determined that the handsome Albert should marry his first cousin, the very fair and very silly Alice Dunbar, chosen pet of the whole race of Dunbars and Millwoods. She was Mrs. Millwood's niece, the daughter of her sister, and a wonderful heiress.

If Mary Etheredge was rich, Alice Dunbar was by many thousands richer, and then Mary's gold was in the fluctuating shape of negroes and crops, while Alice owned whole acres of houses in Broadway, and incalculable shares in the best banks. But Albert defeated all these plans, so well arranged. He would not hear of his cousin Alice. He called her in private to his mother "a mealy-faced doll;" he detested blondes and was desperately in love with his neighbor, the beautiful Ellen Bradway.

Now, if Albert had sought through the wide world, he could not have lighted upon a choice more displeasing to his incensed father. Mr. Bradway was a retired grocer, a man of yesterday, educated at the public expense, who had laboriously worked for and honestly gained a large fortune, a portion of which he invested in the purchase of the next place to Mr. Millwoods on the North River. Of course, the neighbors soon quarreled, that is, Mr. Millwood thought the parvenu a trespasser upon his grounds, and always refused to visit or notice him.

"A fellow like that to own a country seat, which gentlemen have always hitherto occupied. Disgusting!" And he forbade any acquaintance between his family and that of Mr. Bradway. But Mr. Millwood did not recollect that retired grocers, if they are quiet, well-disposed men, and have handsome daughters, get on in the world of New York very comfortably He was destined many times at the finest balls, in what Willis used to call Japonicadom, to meet face to face the detested purchaser of Hilton. Albert was not at any time likely to cling to his father's side at parties, but he very soon learnt to get quite out of sight, for behind window curtains, and in obscure corners, he began to woo the dark-eyed Ellen. John Millwood had been married about four years when matters reached a crisis. Albert was twenty-three—Alice eighteen. "They must be married in April," said Mr. Millwood, "and sail at once for Europe." Albert was told the parental decision, and then he mildly set forth his own notions.

Imagine the rage and astonishment of Mr. Millwood. To have his sage projects disregarded was bad enough, but for his son to espouse the daughter of a grocer! To bring into the family of Millwood a person who had sprung from nothing, the child of a man who had stood behind a counter, and dealt out raisins and figs by the sixpence worth. Never!

Furiously, he commanded Albert either to abandon his intention, and to pay his addresses immediately to his cousin Alice, or else never again to darken his doors with his presence. The consequences may easily be foreseen. The hot-headed youth left the house, and flew to demand Ellen's hand of her father. Mr. Bradway prudently demurred. He could not think of permitting his idolized Ellen to enter a family where she was despised. "Wait," he said, "wait, my dear fellow, your father will come around."

"My father will never come round so long as Alice Dunbar and I are both unmarried. He is more likely to forgive me when he finds the thing is irremediable."

But Mr. Bradway was firm. Albert urged his suit, and Ellen was very much in love, and they were both young and thoughtless, and the "Herald" published the following week the marriage, at Philadelphia, of Albert Millwood, Esq., to Ellen Rosalie, only child of Edward Bradway, Esq., of New York.

The paper lay upon the breakfast table at Mr. Millwood's house, in Murray Street. Alice, who with her mother was spending a few days with her aunt, took it up to read aloud the marriages and deaths for the benefit of Mrs. Dunbar. Albert's name headed the list. Instinctively she stopped at the first word, and, looking very much confused, allowed the paper to fall from her hand.

"Continue, Alice," said the sonorous voice of her stately mother. With a great deal of hesitation, and some slight blushes, Alice complied. Hardly had she reached the middle of the sentence, when poor, delicate Mrs. Millwood, whom a breath of wind laid up with the rheumatism for weeks, and whose nerves were in such a terrible state that she wept herself into convulsions for anybody that chose to call upon her sympathies, fell back in her well-cushioned char, and fainted away.

Mrs. Dunbar, with her pursed-up mouth and brow full of dignity, shook her head ominously, and after protesting that she always knew Albert Millwood would commit some such act, took her daughter's arm and swept majestically from the room. Mary Millwood busied herself with her mother-in-law, and though she pitied and lamented, most sincerely, Albert's rash act (for he was one of her great favorites), she did not dare, openly, to avow her sentiments in the presence of Mr. Millwood. John took up the gazette and read through the announcement with great attention. Mr. Millwood alone remained immovable, and continued to break his dry toast into his tea with seeming indifference. Mrs. Millwood's Abigail arrived in great haste, and after due application of essences and drops her mistress revived.

"What will you do, Mr. Millwood?" she faintly asked, opening her eyes slowly.

"Disinherit him, of course, and never see him again," was the stern reply, as the angry parent stalked from the room, banging the door after him with all that force bangers employ when they wish to express extreme fury. Mr. Millwood kept his word.

Four days after his imprudent match, Albert returned. He asked to see his father. "He is in his study," answered the butler, whom he met in the entry.

Half-fearing, half-hoping, Albert opened the

library door. Mr. Millwood sat in the old chair, his accustomed seat. He looked up as his son entered. With a calm face he rose, extending his hand to the open door. "Leave my sight, young gentleman," he exclaimed, in a steady voice. "You remember our last interview, and my words on that occasion."

Albert turned, and with a lofty step, a proud brow, but a heart almost bursting, sought his mother. As he reached her dressing room door, the sound of a female voice, raised to a high pitch, made him stop. The speaker was his aunt.

"Say what you please, Edith, your son, and my unfortunate nephew, must be far gone indeed, if he dare so openly disobey the express commands of his father. I am happy, though, very happy, that this event has taken place before the marriage of my daughter Alice was decided upon. For, what would have been my feelings, if I had been the unconscious instrument of her future unhappiness?" Here the lady paused, for the simple reason that, having talked herself into a suppressed rage, she feared to continue, lest it should break out.

"Indeed, my dear Charlotte," began her sister, "indeed, Albert never was a bad son."

But the subject of their conversation now considered it time to speak for himself. Opening the door, he entered with a face half sorrowful, half angry. Immediately on perceiving him, Mrs. Dunbar dropped her tapestry-work, and passing her nephew without even a look of recognition, left the dressing room.

"Oh, Albert, Albert!" exclaimed the mother, with strong symptoms of a second *crise de nerfs,* "how could you?"

"Now, mamma, you have not turned against me also?" said the son, stooping to kiss the hand raised with a gesture of expostulation.

"No, my dear boy, but I am afraid your father will never see you again, he is so angry that you did not marry Alice. I am sure I love that sweet girl very much. She always has some of my drops in her workbasket for me, and whenever I have a knot in my embroidery silks, she takes it out. But I don't think, somehow, you would suit."

"Suit, dearest mamma! Why, we never could agree. Alice will be a baby all her life. My gentle aunt has taken such particular pains to bring her up in the way she means to keep her, that I really believe my little cousin would not pretend to say that it was daylight at noon unless the great Charlotte gave her permission. Besides, why do you all talk of my marrying Alice, as if she had no voice in the matter? Alice is not in love with me, poor child! How you all dispose of her! But do not speak to me of such a nonentity, if you could but see my Ellen."

"Oh, that is impossible, Albert. But tell me, what does she look like? I have never seen her, you know."

"Look like? Like everything that is beautiful. Shall I describe her to you, mother?"

He seated himself beside Mrs. Millwood, and taking her hand, began. His voice grew eloquent as he spoke of his bride, as he dwelt upon the luster and radiance of her beauty, the sweetness of her temper and disposition, the wit which sparkled in her conversation, the elegance of her manners; ultimately, not one of her many perfections was forgotten.

An hour passed by, and then, when the footman announced the carriage waiting for Mrs. Millwood's daily drive, her son started up to say farewell.

"Perhaps we may never meet again, dear mother, for, disinherited and disowned, forbidden my father's house, and regarded by all as an outcast, I have no desire to remain much longer in a city which has now become hateful to me. I shall go abroad. Ellen and I can live cheaply in Germany or in Italy."

"Albert, you will not leave us!" said the terrified mother, "I am sure, in a few weeks Mr. Millwood will forget all that has happened, and I shall see my daughter-in-law. Do not leave New York. What will I do without you? Oh, Albert, you will not go!"

"Mother, I will wait three weeks longer here. But if at the end of that time my father continues inexorable, we must part. God grant that we may meet again!"

Hastily embracing her as she clung sobbing to him, he turned to depart.

"Before you go, though, carry at least a bridal present to my daughter." She placed in his hand a small jewel-case. "I meant them for Alice, but never mind. God bless you, my dear boy!" and she sank into her chair, completely overpowered.

Softly and quietly Albert left her, and hardly conscious of what he did, was descending the staircase, when a low voice called gently-

"Albert! Cousin Albert!" Recognizing Alice's voice, he stopped and looked round for her. She stood at the door of the breakfast room, holding it open with one hand, while with the other she extended a small package towards him.

"Do not mention this to any one, Albert. I am,

perhaps, doing very wrong to speak to you, after mamma's having expressly forbidden me to do so, but I cannot let you go away without saying goodbye. Give this to my new cousin. I have heard that she has a beautiful hand, so let her wear this ring for my sake. Goodbye, goodbye! Don't stay any longer, for I hear some one coming down stairs." She flung the little bundle at his feet, closed the door, and Albert saw her for the last time. Hastily raising this second gift, he left the house with a rapid step, never again to return.

Ellen was waiting anxiously for him. She was sitting in a splendidly furnished drawing room, her father opposite her, and both talking earnestly. Mr. Bradway had been easily reconciled to his only child; and, as Albert had always been a favorite, he had immediately pardoned and received the rash but repentant couple. Ellen heard her husband's step, and with a beating heart ran to meet him.

"What success, my dear boy?" inquired the kind, good old man, grasping his son-in-law's hand. All was told, in a few words. Ellen burst into tears, and burying her head upon her father's shoulder, wept bitterly.

"Come, cheer up, my own!" exclaimed Mr. Bradway. "Am I not rich enough for us three?

Albert is my own son, and, in spite of everything, we shall yet be happy."

"And Ellen, see, my dear mother and sweet cousin have both sent 'gifts to deck the bride.'" He opened the case which Mrs. Millwood had given him, and took out a magnificent *parure* of opals, with which he forthwith decorated his fair Ellen. Then, placing Alice's ring upon her finger, he gently drew her towards the mirror, and called her attention to the rich luster of the gems.

CHAPTER III.

The three weeks having elapsed, and Mr. Millwood still remaining insensible to the tears and prayers of the whole family, Albert began to prepare for his departure. Mr. Bradway was to remain in New York for the purpose of settling some business affairs, and expected to join his children in the course of a month. They left New York and arrived at Paris, where for a few days nothing was talked of but the beauty and grace of the lovely American. At the appointed time Mr. Bradway joined them. Their hotel was one of the handsomest in Paris. They lived in great splendor for about two years, and then went to Italy. At Naples they now established themselves permanently, and their happiness was rendered complete by the birth of a daughter.

This child, to whom Albert gave his mother's name of Edith, was nearly fourteen years old when a great change fell upon the hitherto prosperous family. Mr. Bradway, though his nominal home was with his daughter, in Italy, nevertheless passed many months in his own country. He was a successful speculator. He amused himself by dabbling in stocks, railway shares and so on. There arrived the troubles and disasters which desolated New York, and he was among the first, as he also was among the heaviest losers. The rumor reached Albert before the official intelligence. Mr. Bradway was in despair. They hastened to comfort him, and, after fifteen years' absence, once more the Millwods set foot upon their native land. With energy and decision Albert undertook the arrangement of his father-in-law's difficulties, and from the wreck of a hardly-earned affluence succeeded in rescuing about ten thousand dollars.

Mr. Bradway could not recover from the shock. He was old. He grew nervous. He would take his little granddaughter on his knee and look intently at her for hours, murmuring quietly, "Poor Edith, what a different fate I thought yours would be!"

"Come, sir!" Albert would say, "it is not so bad, after all. I must begin to work. I have played gentleman too long for a sober republican. Edith will be an heiress yet, like her mother before her."

But the old man would shake his head mournfully; and in the end he died two months after his failure. His life appeared to have been bound up in his fortune, and could not survive it.

The Millwoods established themselves very modestly in New York, and Albert sought a basis for the erection of that heiresship which he promised to his daughter. His father was still alive, but neither the prosperity of his undutiful son, nor his present adversity, changed in the slightest degree his feelings towards him: he refused to see him. Mrs. Millwood was dead. John had several children, and was friendly enough, in an economical way, to his younger brother.

"It is hard luck, Al, my boy," John said, one day as the brothers were walking up Broadway, a short time after Mr. Bradway's death, "but my father can't forgive you. Alice's fortune going out of the family cut him to the soul. He never sees William Hamilton, the happy husband of our cousin, without experiencing an accession of bile. And far from being touched by this sad business of poor Bradway, it has only added, if possible, to his still rankling ire."

"Well, John," said Albert, forcing a smile, "my only hope is in you."

John Millwood fidgeted. "There's the rub, my dear fellow. The very day that my father heard of Mr. Bradway's failure, and of the approaching sale of Hilton, so soon as the Gordon's lease is out, he called me up and said, "I will buy Hilton and settle it at once upon you, if you will swear, never with one penny of my money or of your wife's, to assist the man who calls himself Albert Millwood. No gold of mine shall serve to reward him for his disobedience, or to keep the grandchildren of a pitiful dealer in groceries from starvation.""

"And you consented of course!" said Albert.

"What could I do, Al? The old gentleman went on to say that, if I hesitated, he would alter his will on the spot, and leave his entire estate to my children, making me, so far as his property was concerned, dependent upon them."

The younger brother made no remark.

"And you see, Albert, I have a very small income from Mary's plantation, after all. I can't live at the South, it kills me. I hate negroes. I can't manage them, and the estate doesn't yield us what it ought to do. Then we have three children, and may have more, and New York is such an extravagant city, and—"

"Say no more, dear John. Enough of all this. I would not for millions stand in the way of your interests. goodbye; Ellen is waiting for me, and she is not well."

"Mary is coming to see her and your little girl," exclaimed John.

"No, she must not take that trouble. Ellen sees no one at present, and though Mrs. John Millwood would pass for a sister in the register of our births, John, still fifteen years is such a long stretch that family affection dries out. I am afraid that Ellen would look upon my brother's wife as an utter stranger. Goodbye."

Albert shook John's hand. Did either guess that that hasty grasp was the last they would ever exchange?

Albert fancied he would get on better in Baltimore. They moved there, and Ellen's health failed. Physicians were called in: "Mrs. Millwood had lived too long in Italy, in no other climate would they answer for her life."

That was decisive; back they went to the sunny

skies which the now fragile wife longed for.
Gradually, of course, the ten thousand dollars
melted away, though they exercised the strictest
economy. At length, when Edith was sixteen, at the
beginning of October, the still beautiful Ellen
Bradway fell into her long sleep, leaving husband
and child most desolate.

There was no reason for remaining idle and
unhappy in ungrateful Italy, which could not save
the dearly loved. So they buried their dead, and
came back to America.

Few could have recognized the pale, elderly,
careworn man, who with a tall girl in the deepest
mourning on his arm, roamed the streets of New
York, looking for cheap lodgings, as the once
handsome and dashing Albert Millwood.

Twice in the course of that winter John Millwood,
in stepping from his admirably built wagon to enter
some grand shop in Broadway, brushed against a
rather shabbily-got-up person, who, with books
under his arm, was hastening into a side street. The
first time it occurred the stranger looked up, and
something in his eyes, or in the turn of his brow,
made the rich son of a millionaire father start. But
the foot passenger glanced indifferently at wagon,
horse, and owner, and the flush passed from John

Millwood's forehead as he muttered, "Good God! What a likeness. But this man is ten years older than Albert, and Albert is abroad."

The next time they met at the same spot, but a find youth of nineteen or twenty was framing some request about "a day's sport over on Long Island," and Mr. Millwood's attention was taken up by this noble-looking eldest son.

Of course it was Albert, and the books he had under his arm he was carrying home to Edith, who eked out their slender means by translating French, German, or Italian stories at the will of her employers. Under the name of Woodville, Albert was clerk in an importing house, and thus they managed to live. He would have perished on the rack, rather than have asked for help from his family. But, alas! They had not reached the end of their trials. The father sickened. Whether a broken heart is really a disease of which people die, or whether it generates other ills, Albert Millwood was dying. Too weak at last to go to the counting house, he was forced to resign his post. The firm civilly hoped that their hard-working clerk might recover his health and return to them. They knew nothing of him, except that his recommendation came from their attorney, a certain Edward Stockton, who had been absent for some months at the South. When her father gave up his clerkship, Edith began to give French and music lessons at a third-rate boarding school. At night she still translated. At odd hours she copied music, or painted hand-screens, or even embroidered muslins and scalloped flannels for a fashionable baby warehouse. So the winter dragged along. Spring brought no light to Albert Millwood's eyes, no health to his wan cheek, no comfort to his aching heart. He was patient and very sorrowful.

He watched Edith with such intense anxiety that he was restless when her school duties called her away. There was such a charm in the uncomplaining cheerfulness of that young and beautiful creature, who, if she did sometimes breathe a sigh at her hard lot, never let its uttered regret reach her father's ear.

The Easter holiday, late that year, came at last, but Mr. Millwood was so ill that Edith did not dare to send away the nurse, who only attended when she was with her pupils.

It was on the Wednesday of Easter week that Albert Millwood died. On Thursday he was buried; and it was on Friday, therefore, that Edith sat before her father's desk, and read what might be considered his last will and testament. This was it:

"The time has come, my child, and we must part.

It will be easier to tell you goodbye, on this paper, than with your hand in mine. You will, perhaps, be busy with your scholars when my hour comes; so take now, my darling, my blessing and my farewell. You have been very, very good. Few girls of sixteen could have gone through your trials without sinking under them. You have wonderful steadiness, energy, and courage for your years. God is very merciful. He took from me family, fortune, wife, health, but he has left me a daughter like you and one true friend. Is the man miserable who can say as much? Mr. Stockton is your guardian, Edith, and though you have never yet seen him, already he loves you, and but for this important business at Mobile, he would long since have been here. I expect him daily. I should be very glad to meet him before I die. He was your grandfather's warmest friend, and his love for the Bradway's descended to me. Mr. Stockton wishes you to live with him. He is a bachelor, has no immediate family, and makes a moderate income from his profession. Decide for yourself, but I should almost wish that you might remain independent. However, exercise your own good sense and judgement; receive Mr. Stockton as one whom you know and appreciate; listen to his advice, ponder well all that he says. I never have talked to you about this, for you shrink so naturally from hearing me discuss what will come after an event you foresee and dread. I can write no more. My hand is tired, and my brain swims with this unaccustomed work. God bless you, my poor Edith. Recollect that, 'He tempers the wind to the shorn lamb.'"

The orphan's tears fell fast upon this sacred paper, which she read many times before it was folded and put away. Mr. Stockton's name was not new to her. She remembered having seen him, though her father had forgotten it. It was nearly four years back, when they first returned from abroad, and she had yet in her possession a little carved ivory needle-case which he had then presented to her, while she sat as usual beside he grandfather's knee. Albert Millwood had grown latterly a very silent man. He had received but one letter from Mr. Stockton, during the last sad winter, and after mentioning it casually to Edith, they did not speak again on the subject. Having decided upon her course, he had accepted Mr. Stockton's offer of her guardianship; but he had postponed telling her of it, knowing that few words were necessary at any time for her direction, and that in any event his written wishes would be decisive with her.

Three weeks passed, and Edith was beginning to wonder when her guardian would appear. At length she was summoned one morning from her school. A gentleman was waiting for her, and begged that Mrs. Callender, the head of the establishment, would kindly spare Miss Woodville. The visitor was sitting in Mrs. Twiggs' little parlor. He rose at Edith's entrance, a tall, grave, gentlemanly man of fifty, and folded in his arms the pale mourner, who nervously and tremblingly recognized Mr. Stockton.

"I am here at last, my child," he said in a most kind voice: "how I have longed to be here!"

"How I have longed for you, sir," said Edith. "If you could have been with us, before he, my father —" and an uncontrollable burst of tears finished the sentence.

Mr. Stockton gently removed the heavy veil and close black bonnet of his ward. He let her weep in peace, and after a few moments she looked up and said, I am not always so weak."

"I would not have you stronger, Edith. While Mrs. Twiggs' little girl has been in search of you, I have been talking to your landlady, and though I cannot but admire your steady determination to conquer all useless grief, still you have kept your sorrow too much pent up. It is hurtful to do such

violence to your feelings. Mrs. Callender would
surely have spared you a few days after Easter. But
now are you ready to go home with me? Time
enough to scold you, when we are safe at home."

At home, sir?"

"Yes, at my snug, unostentatious little home,
where Hardy, my housekeeper, has had your room
prepared these two hours, and where, without
waiting for your kind permission, I shall instantly
convey you and your trunks. There comes our hack,
rattling to the door, and here is our friend Mrs.
Twiggs ready to help you.

Smiling Mrs. Twiggs, grieved to lose her lodger,
but really pleased at "sweet Miss Woodville actually
having somebody to take care of her, and such a real
gentleman too;—paid the rent, and with something
over to the bargain," as she afterwards told her
neighbor Mrs. Tucker, "saying 'twas little enough, if
I was kind to the poor gentleman and his daughter."
Mrs. Twiggs eagerly assisted in the packing of
Edith's property.

The hackman pronounced his vehicle adequate
for the conveyance of almost everything; a box or
two remained behind for future removal, and then,
with a thousand blessings from her landlady, and
eyes once more overflowing past control, Edith was

handed to the carriage by her guardian.

CHAPTER IV.

"Now, my dear Edith," said Mr. Stockton, when, the cloth having been removed after dinner, the two sat alone in the pleasant dining room of her new home—"Now my dear, since you have seen your whole establishment, since you have professed yourself satisfied with the appearance of Hardy the housekeeper, of Jane our waitress, and have enjoyed the simple efforts of Sarah the cook; since you have tried the piano in the front parlor, looked over my little library, and settled yourself in your own especial chintz-hung bower up stairs; since you have examined me carefully and furtively from beneath the shadow of those long black eyelashes, yes, I have watched you, tell me, now, if you think you can be contented here?"

"Contented, my dear sir, who could not be? I ought to be very happy, but not just yet. How kind you are to m."

"Then you are willing to give up the pleasure of passing half your days at Mrs. Callender's?"

"Oh no!" said Edith earnestly. "Your roof and home are indeed blessings which I should never dream of thanking you for and declining. But I must not, cannot be a dependent altogether. I have health, and youth, and strength. Why should I be an idler?"

"You will not be an idler, my child. You shall practice a great deal, and read a great deal, and draw, and do worsted work, and knit woolen socks for me, if you choose, and every evening you shall sing me to sleep, or charm me wide awake with your singing."

Edith shook her head.

"Then you shall write my friendly letters, and pay the visits I ought to pay to my dowager clients, and be in fact a very busy, and hardly worked little creature."

"Read this, sir," was Edith's answer. She gave him her father's letter. Mr. Stockton read it, and after a pause went on.

"I shall say no more, my dear, do as you think best. But I have, you know, even through this letter, a legal claim to direct and guide you. For the present, I forbid any fulfillment of your engagements with Mrs. Callender. During this summer you must rest, and recover your plumpness, and color. You have been overtasked, your poor father wrote me that not six weeks ago. Why you are as thin as a starved chicken, and have no more red in your cheeks than remains on the face of a much washed alabaster doll. We will go to some quiet farmhouse in July, and stay there till October. Then my child, if you still wish to prove me unnecessary to you, you may recommence your instructions in *sol-fas* and *parlez-vous.*"

Mr. Stockton took her hand, for Edith had risen from her seat, and was standing beside him, very mournful but very resolute. "You don't have to choose to owe me any thing, yet you ought to feel that your presence is ample return for your board and lodging. Ah, the blood of the Millwoods! Ah, the proud blood of the Millwoods!"

Edith started as if she had been stung. "I am no Millwood, sir. I acknowledge no blood of theirs— even my dear father disavowed them. My name is

Woodville. He died a Woodville, an assumed name, no name at all, but still, one, which I cherish more than that of Millwood. They let him die, alone, poor, while his brother and his father lived not one mile from him. I have seen those Millwoods in the street, at a distance. They are a cold, heartless, frozen race. I am no Millwood. I shall live and die as Edith Woodville."

The girl was transformed. Her large eyes flashed and glowed, her white cheek crimsoned, and her tall, slight figure towered like the proud young thing she was—deeply offended and resentful.

"Forgive me, dear Mr. Stockton," she presently continued, softening down, though her bosom still heaved, "you see what an uncomfortable child I am." And she kissed her guardian's hand, which a moment before she had thrown from her.

Mr. Stockton patted the bowed head, which seemed quite ashamed of its own violence, and changed the conversation.

"Have you any young acquaintances? Any female friends, my dear, whom you would like to inform of your change of residence?"

"I!" exclaimed Edith, "none, sir. We lived so alone, so apart from the world, that, except to my landlady, and occasionally to one of her lodgers, when we met on the stairs, I have spoken to no creature beyond my scholars and my employer."

The evening gradually closed in. Edith made an effort to sing—the first time since her father's death —and her guardian was amazed at her talent, even heard under such disadvantage. She was a rare creature, this forsaken offshoot of a proud family. Her education had been conducted with the utmost care, and till their misfortunes came, her parents had spared no expense to render her a most accomplished woman. Living after that entirely with her mother, whose mind was of the highest order, Edith was as much advanced in knowledge and character as any well-developed girl of twenty. The sorrows which had fallen in such quick succession upon her young head had necessarily aided to mature her. She was singularly self-possessed, and, though cheerful, seldom happy.

Her life now passed quietly, yet to her most pleasantly. Nothing more was said, either by Mr. Stockton or by herself, about her future plans. Few words sufficed for both of them. It was to be as he had determined. During this summer her time belonged to him. She rose early, made her guardian's breakfast, consulted a little with Mrs. Hardy, and then devoted her hours till dinner to music and study. Towards the twilight of these bright days of late spring, they would go out for a long stroll in the least-frequented squares. Many inquiring looks were directed by Mr. Stockton's passing acquaintances to the graceful figure and closely-veiled face of the unknown lady on his arm. To those who afterwards asked about her, the story was very simple: she was his ward, left to his charge by her deceased father, "who had known better days." They had always lived abroad, and their name was Woodville. Some few sneerers and scandalmongers, at first, pretended to smile and look knowing; but their congratulations on his good fortune met with such a reception that the boldest never dared a repetition. One or two quiet men of his own age occasionally dined in Ninth Street, and were welcomed by Edith as hostess. It so chanced that several times her grandfather's name was mentioned, by one or other of these gentlemen. Once a Mr. Lawrence spoke of Albert Millwood, and remarked that he seemed to have disappeared from view altogether. Edith did not betray herself. She was determined that her father's people should never by any possibility learn her existence. She would never permit them, by some trifling act of charity offered to herself, to persuade their easy

consciences that they had atoned for their
unkindness to their son and brother.

The wives and daughters of these guests called
upon Miss Woodville, but her deep mourning did
not permit a return of their civility. She did not
"take" to any of them. Consequently she lived
almost as much retired now as she had done during
the winter.

In July they moved into the country. Edith grew
strong, and gained so many pounds that her
guardian was delighted. It charmed him to see her
each day blooming into new beauty. If she laughed
or jested, he listened with such pleasure to her pure,
fresh voice. Any girlish trick or speech seemed
quite like a *chef-d'œuvre* of his own creation, it was
so great a change from her previous self.

But October came, and Mr. Stockton began to
look grave, and they were back in Ninth Street.
Edith soberly said, one evening, "Dear Guardy, I am
going to set to work."

"Are you still resolved?"

"Quite resolved."

"I have an offer to make you, Edith. A plan which
I prefer to yours, though I shall be still more a loser
by it. There is a young widow, a very charming
woman, who has no children, and no agreeable aunt

or maiden sister to live with her. She feels solitary
in her large house; and being a client of mine, and a
very good friend besides, she has been consulting
me about getting a companion. Not a husband, alas!
For that, poor thing! Is impossible, as I will tell you
presently. She wishes an accomplished and sweet-
tempered creature of the softer sex. One clever
enough and chatty enough to be a desirable inmate,
and yet one who won't talk her to death. She wishes
a young girl, but not a frivolous bread-and-butter
miss. She wishes an excellent musician, but a
person who can think of something besides pianos
and hard-strings. She wishes a ladylike and pleasing
occupant for the other back seat of her carriage, but
not a flaunting dresser, who will torture her good
taste by a profusion of reds and yellows. In a word,
she wishes to procure, for the handsome sum of six
hundred dollars per annum, a nice girl, acquainted
with modern languages, who can conduct herself
with modesty and propriety—make music when
required, write notes, read aloud, 'play watch-dog to
keep off the wolves,' and not look dowdy when
seen abroad or at home."

Edith's lip curled.

"Do you propose me as this paragon, sir? I would
rather teach little Betty Thompson the verb '*avoir*,

to have," or induct Miss Cleopatra Mills, the elegant daughter of the restaurant-keeper, into the mysteries of 'that sweet thing of Herz,' than dance attendance upon a New York find lady as her *souffre douleur,* with her cast-off gowns for my perquisites."

"Not so fast, my darling. Wait till you see Mrs. Stratford. She is not a fine lady; she is a warm-hearted, right-feeling little woman, who has had a hard life. Did you not hear my 'alas!' just now? She was married to a man who could not appreciate, and badly treated her. He died some time ago—she has just dropped her weeds—leaving her, it is true, his immense fortune, but on one condition: that she should not remarry. She is about twenty-five, and without many near relatives, sees stretching before her a long vista of solitary years. She will always be exposed to unkind remarks. Very few choose to believe that a widow, without children, young and attractive, can live without love. She has been, and will be constantly, accused of clandestine admirers or clandestine marriages. No behavior of hers can prevent the slander. Let her life privately—'all the more convenient for *carryings-on*;' let her rush about in the full glare of the world—every second man she speaks to is pointed out as 'the happy fellow.' This is what a selfish man entails upon the wife he leaves behind him."

Edith was interested. "Is she petty, this very rich yet unhappily situated widow?"

"You shall see her and judge for yourself. All the summer she has been at Newport, but last week she came to town, and we have been speaking on the subject of this wished-for companion. I do not fear for you in being with her. After all, she has so much good sense, and so much weight in society, that her position is better than almost any woman's would be, under the same circumstances."

"You have not offered me to her," said Edith, with slight displeasure.

"I took no such liberty with your exalted majesty," replied Mr. Stockton, laughing "how ungrateful you are, little Edith! Do you consider that by placing you in this grand house, I shall lose your sweet smile which illumines this humble one; for if I permitted you to devote your energies to Betty Thompson, and to the elegant Miss Cleopatra, I should still have you to pour out my tea, and to tell me good night, as you now must do, for it is eleven o'clock," and the kind guardian lighted her bedroom candle, kissed her white forehead, and opened the door with old-fashioned courtesy. "Think over my plan, dear, and pleasant dreams."

CHAPTER V.

"Miss Woodville and Mr. Stockton," announced the footman. Mrs. Stratford came forward with the kindest welcome. Her handsome suite of drawing rooms opened into such a little chamber, as in novels would be called a "boudoir," and there she was sitting. It was all made up of rose-colored silk and soft lace coverings, with white and gilded furniture. A single large window overlooked a kind of hanging garden, which was only a small enclosed balcony, filled with geraniums, heliotrope and mignonette. Though the day was cool, the sash was folded back, and this miniature conservatory sent forth from its simple treasures a balmy sweetness that filled the air. The opposite side of the room was paneled with one entire mirror. A portrait of a beautiful girl in an oval frame held the place of honor above the low chimney-piece, which overshadowed a little fireplace, fit for a doll's house, and of which the *irons* were misnomers, for they looked as if no such vulgar metal had assisted in their manufacture. The prettiest knick-knacks of the daintiest style abounded. It was a little bower for a little fairy.

Mrs. Stratford seemed made for her boudoir, as her boudoir was made for her. She was slight, delicate, fragile, with a hand and foot never before seen out of Lilliput. She was not thin, for her round waist showed no flatness, and her shoulders were so perfectly moulded that you guessed their plump contour through her morning dress. She was fair, with a bright color, very large, affectionate eyes, dark hair, and a mouth of the sweetest expression. She was not beautiful, but *very* lovable. The most curious thing about her was the dignity of her figure and manner, though she had neither height not coldness.

Without closely examining Edith, Mrs. Stratford managed to criticize her carefully, and an approving nod to Mr. Stockton was her first signal of commendation. Presently my heroine moved nearer the chimney, to look at the portrait to which her guardian called her attention. The light fell full upon her face, just as she turned her eyes towards him, and Mrs. Stratford was astonished at her beauty.

"That is Miss Florence Tremaine, Mrs. Stratford's niece," said Mr. Stockton, and he began to ask about her and to draw out their hostess. He had no fear of Mrs. Stratford's impression of Edith. He wished Edith to be pleased with Mrs. Stratford.

And Edith was pleased. There was a simplicity, a kindness, an honesty, in Clara Stratford which went straight to the hearts of those who were capable of understanding her. She was not clever, she never said a brilliant thing, but she appreciated wit in others, and making no attempt to shine, always satisfied. When she spoke, her friends listened, for her words were sure to convey a right and proper sentiment. She thought much, she never chattered.

After a half hour's visit the guests rose to take their leave. Then Mrs. Stratford held Edith's hand and said,

"Let us be frank, Miss Woodville, will you accept my offer? I find you just what I expected!"

"Yes," said Edith, simply.

"Thank you! When will you come to me—tomorrow?"

Edith looked at her guardian. He gravely bowed.

"Tomorrow then," decided Mrs. Stratford, and she rang the bell.

"I like her very much," said Edith, as they walked down the Fifth Avenue, for, of course, the rich widow lived in that splendid quarter. "I am willing to be her companion, but," she went on, "I do grieve to leave you."

Mr. Stockton pressed the little gloved hand that rested on his arm, and said:

"It is true—you can't help it. I know I drive you from me. I am a heartless old cynic, who detests the sight of fair young faces, eh, Edith? It is I who insist upon your glorious independence."

Hardy, the housekeeper, could not understand Miss Edith's going away. There was a jeremiad of lamentations raised throughout the establishment, and when the carriage came to the door after dinner the next day, one would have thought the respectable hack was either a disguised hearse or a convict's cart.

Mr. Stockton left her at Mrs. Stratford's door. "God bless you, my Edith. Remember this is not your home. At the end of a year I shall reclaim you. Should you return to me before that time, how fondly you will be welcomed."

The true woman spoke in Edith's answer. "Don't get accustomed to my absence, sir. Pray miss me a little. And, oh Guardy, come to see me very, very often."

Marshaled through the lofty passage and up a grand staircase, Edith met Mrs. Stratford on the first landing of the bedroom corridor. She was wrapped in her dressing gown.

"I expected you much earlier, Miss Woodville," she kindly said, "and hoped to install you comfortably myself, but now I shall have to depute that office to Léonide," and she glanced towards her maid. "I forgot yesterday that I had an engagement this evening, for which I am now dressing in all haste. You will see your room, and then I will beg you to do me a favor. I expect a friend, the original of the portrait you so much admired yesterday—my niece. I got a note from her this morning. She will be here tonight, and you must receive her for me. Léonide, conduct Mademoiselle. *Sans adieu.*"

The fluttering little Frenchwoman threw open the bedroom door. It was spacious, handsomely furnished, and boasted every newly invented luxury.

Mlle. Léonide bustled about, removed Edith's hat
and shawl, lighted the wax tapers on the dressing
table, pushed forward an arm chair, inquired in
authoritative tones from a passing chamber maid
"why Mademoiselle's trunks were not brought up,"
and made Edith quite nervous with her fidgetings.

At length all was arranged to suit Léonide's
fancy, and with a tripping curtsey she took her
leave.

Edith sat down before the mirror to smooth her
hair, but the brush soon fell from her listless hand,
and she dreamed away for several minutes. Did she
see reflected on that polished surface a face and
figure almost unrivaled? Edith's eyes were of a
bluish gray, with lashes so long and black that they
cast a shadow upon her cheek. The eyebrows were
like a pencilled thread, not very arched, but setting
their mark firmly upon her somewhat low, broad
forehead. Her skin was smooth as a child's, and so
purely white that is reminded one of snowy rose
leaf, it was so fresh and colorless. Her nose was
slightly aquiline, with a thin, high-bred nostril that
quivered when she spoke with emotion. Her mouth,
with a very short upper lip, was so red, that it was
almost a peculiarity in her face. It seemed too
trenchant upon the whiteness of her cheek and teeth.

Her hair had possibly the same fault of glaring contrast; for no Indian maiden's cherished locks were ever darker or more luxuriant. Edith wore it like two shining bands of black satin, folded away from her small ears, and wound smoothly at the back, over an exquisitely carved jet comb, her guardian's gift, and the only ornament of her dress. Her well-shaped head was balanced upon a throat, delicate and nicely turned, like a sculptor's masterpiece. Exquisitely proportioned, her figure, above the middle height, was neither fat nor thin, it was so admirably moulded. It was like a strain of perfect music, undulating, easy, and graceful. The whole expression of Edith's person was a reading of herself. It was softened pride, a lofty spirit, yet a gentle heart. She blushed when startled or hurt, but her head never lost its regal carriage, and the movement of her hands and arms she might have learned from Le Clairon in her most queenly roles.

Edith's musings did not continue long. They were not pleasant ones, so she banished them, arranged her simple dress, searched for her work-box, and prepared to begin her life of servitude by proceeding to the drawing room to wait the arrival of Miss Tremaine.

The carriage was waiting for Mrs. Stratford, but

she had not yet come down. Suddenly a sharp ring at the street bell was followed by a little bustle. The drawing room door opened quickly, and in walked Miss Tremaine, her hat falling from her head, and the folds of a muddy skirt gather up in her hand.

"Here I am, Aunt Clara," she exclaimed, but seeing only the unknown figure in black, sitting at a sofa-table, she slightly bowed, and, reopening the door, called to a footman: "Thomas, where is Mrs. Stratford?"

"In her room, ma'am, and she gives orders you would be pleased to come there."

At this instant, Mrs. Stratford, radiant in jewels and dress, came down the stairs. "Ah, Florence, I am very glad you have at last arrived," she said, tenderly embracing her. "What has kept you? How cold your hands are! Come in."

"In a second—Thomas, pray see that Ann has someone to help with my luggage. In the name of ghosts, who is that fair apparition?" she continued, in a low tone.

"My new *dame de compagnie*—but not an ordinary one. Miss Woodville, this is, as you may have guessed, my niece, Miss Tremaine," said Mrs. Stratford, as she presented the girls to each other.

Florence was not more than six years younger

than her twenty-five year old aunt. She was the daughter of a step-sister of Clara's. Her mother died when she was born, and Mr. Tremaine had married again, and lived in the West. Florence was the peculiar charge of Miss Manvers, another sister of Mrs. Stratford by her father's first marriage, and Miss Tremaine alone came on visits to her youthful aunt. But between them they managed to make these visits very long, and the intervals very short. Florence looked like Clara, but was larger and more showy, very lively, and had no pretensions to steadiness.

"You're beautiful, little Clara," she exclaimed, *en français,* as she spread out the flounces of Mrs. Stratford's beautiful pink silk dress, all finished off with wide point lace corresponding to her shawl, "and who will drown tonight, lost by the brilliance of your eyes?"

"Florence always speaks French, when she is impertinent," said Mrs. Stratford, smiling at Edith. "I am going to take a cup of tea first with you, and then I call at the Lewis Summers' to bid them goodbye, after which I have promised to look in at a small party given to some Southerners, by Mrs. Hall."

"What dissipation! Especially the tea with us. But

I don't know, I think a sleep on one of Mrs. Hall's sofas while the hostess is talking to you may rank as the most overpowering excitement. But you don't ask the why of my muddied skirt, and of my late arrival?"

"But I wish to know very much?"

"Well, I have had an accident and an adventure."

"Both! Fortunately here comes the tea-tray to support us if your narrative is too harrowing."

"Oh, it is very interesting," said Florence, with a mischievous look. "Aunt Margaret's two fat horses were leisurely whisking their tails, and peaceably trotting at a dowager pace along the road this afternoon, and I was giving Ann, my Abigail, a lecture which ought to have been bestowed upon her two weeks since, when suddenly, in the midst of a sentence—causing me to bite my tongue, so unexpected was it,—down we came—the linch-pin or axle-tree, or—the coachman knows what, had given way, and there I was, disconsolately seated. Ann was screaming, and Aunt Margaret's cherished equipage all on one side. "

"Were you hurt at all?" said Clara, anxiously.

"Not a bit, only the bitten tongue. I scrambled out of the door, soiled my dress in the effort, ordered Ann to cease her shrieks, and began consulting with

the coachman and footman. So far, you perceive
nothing romantic, but to prove that chivalry is not
quite extinct, a gallant knight sprang, not from his
war-horse but from his inglorious trotting wagon,
and rushed to my assistance. He gathered me up,
quieted Ann, and he dispatched John to the nearest
house, which fortunately was close at hand, and
after an hour's delay we were once more ready to
start. I 'thanked my preserver,' pursued my perilous
journey, and you see me now."

"Who was your knight?"

"Mr. Edward Curtis; he came to town yesterday.
He says, by the way, that he will call here
tomorrow. Don't blush, Aunt Clara."

"Florence," exclaimed Mrs. Stratford, glancing
towards Edith, "how did you leave my sister
Margaret?" she continued.

Florence laughed saucily. "Your sister Margaret is
in the rudest health. She has charged me with a
package for you, of no small dimensions, and such
volumes of messages relating to my manners,
morals and conduct, that fearing I should partially
and disrespectfully forget some, I have concluded
not to remember any. She says I must stay a very
little while and come back immediately. My
determination is to stay a very long while, and not

to go back at all. It is so dull at Ravenswood. Who but Aunt Margaret would dream of staying all the year round in the country, when one lives within eighteen miles of dear New York, and of such a dear Clara?"

Mrs. Stratford kissed the spoiled beauty: Léonide, with a sweeping salutation to Miss Tremaine and a face all smiles, appeared with her mistress's shawl. "Good night, Miss Woodville. Florence, don't sit up late. Be very kind to her," she whispered in her niece's ear, as they left the room together, Mrs. Stratford to fulfill her evening's engagements, and Florence to change her dress.

On her return, before very long she and Edith were on the best possible terms. Florence had her aunt's frankness and candor, with her own sprightliness and quick feelings. Her likings were sudden, but not the less lasting on that account. She was too amiable to be jealous of Edith's evident superiority in all the accomplishments they talked of, and in all the knowledge of books with which she herself was unacquainted, and she was too handsome and too much admired to dread "a rival near the throne." She admired her vastly from the first moment, and wondered what her talents, without in the least depreciating them. They had no mutual friends; Edith knew no watering-place gossip, so that they sang for each other, and discoursed about things, not people. Miss Woodville was likewise quite carried away by her new acquaintance. She did not generally approve of "lively girls," she thought them a "sad bore," but Florence was not of this usual sort. They took to each other at once—the night melted away and to their surprise before they could believe it, bedtime.

"Aunt Clara would scold if she knew that I had disobeyed her parting injunction. She is such a dragon," said Florence laughing, as she rang to order the lights put out. "What a voice you have, Miss Woodville! I hope I shall still hear it in my dreams."

CHAPTER VI.

Edith's duties were pleasant and varied. Besides the work which her guardian had half-jestingly detailed to her, she gave a Spanish lesson to both ladies daily, and occasionally the giddy Florence would ask to receive some instruction in music. Gradually the humble position of the companion rose into the dignity and distinction of a friend. It came about very naturally; mistress and servants, without intending it, bowed to the native high breeding of Edith; and she herself had unconsciously such a grand air, that from the beginning no one had treated her like a hired dependent. She had claims besides, as Mr. Stockton's ward, to be considered in the light of a lady, and before she had slept a week under Mrs. Stratford's roof, Clara began to behave to her very much as she did to her niece. Mr. Stockton was formally invited to dine every Sunday, and it pleased him very much to see the terms upon which they so soon stood.

"You have given me a pearl, my dear sir," Mrs. Stratford, sometimes would say.

"Lent, not given, my dear madam," always corrected the gentleman.

Florence was enthusiastic about her. Even severe Miss Manvers, who had come to town on a day's visit, was impressed by the quiet, graceful propriety of the young girl.

"I like you, my dear," she said. "I don't like many people, but you are to my taste. I am glad to have you with Florence," and she kissed her. A wonderful demonstration for Aunt Margaret!

Edith generally walked with Mrs. Stratford or with Florence, and sometimes drove with them. But she did not, of course, go to the opera or theaters, or to make visits. Her mourning was too deep for the two first; and, beautiful and noble-looking as she was, no one called on her, or thought of so doing.

When she first appeared in Broadway, in a closely-fitting walking-dress of black cloth, and a small black bonnet, serving as a frame to her pure oval face, with its deep raven bandeaux, its red lips, and its large eyes, she attracted no small attention.

"Who is that superb creature all dressed in black, like one of Malbrook's followers?" said a pretty little woman.

"She steps like an empress," said a novel-reading youth.

"Nonsense! She steps like my fast trotter, Flight, and that is more to the purpose," said "Young New York," lost in admiration.

The answer soon came—"a humble companion of Mrs. Stratford's- the sheep-dog, you know;" for everybody reads Becky Sharp.

Edith's train dropped off. The women were well pleased to find out the stranger's belongings. She could be no rival of theirs; no man cared to know more of her. She did not look coquettish. She did not look "fast." There was nothing encouraging in her stately carriage.

"Would you like me to present you to Miss Woodville?" asked Florence, when young Woodbury inquired who was Miss Tremaine's lovely friend. They were standing in Stewart's famous shop, and Edith was helping Mrs. Stratford to choose embroideries, while Florence chatted with her last night's partner, whom she endured because she thought him good-natured.

"Ya'as, please do. Is she staying with you?"

"She is my aunt's companion, and charming beyond description."

"Oh, just so," drawled out Augustus; "some other time, Miss Tremaine. Ah! I see Bob Bellamy across the street. Good morning. I have an engagement with him." It took Augustus a long time to understand why Florence Tremaine never danced with him again.

But this hint, and a few others, coming from ladies who cooly bowed to Edith on being introduced, and as coolly cut her whenever they could afterwards, taught Florence that unless she wished to narrow down the circle of her acquaintance to a very small ring indeed, by snubbing those who snubbed her friend, she must let the world take its own course, and let it ignore entirely a charming girl, because she was poor, and chose to accept an honest sum for honest services.

Edith did not at first perceive that she was not considered fit company for the fine ladies and "fast men." *She* did not admire *them*, and if she happened

to be in the drawing room when visitors were
announced, unless Mrs. Stratford desired her to stay,
she generally retired.

At length it dawned upon her. But I am sorry to
confess, that my heroine was so vain, she felt
neither sorrow nor mortification. She only drew
herself still more into her shell, and when
accidentally thrown with them, never spoke, but
diligently threaded her worsted needles or cut her
pencils, as if she had been quite alone.

One day, a lady who had been markedly rude to
Edith, heard her sing. She was getting up a little
party and this new voice would be a feature. With
consummate effrontery, she invited Edith to
accompany Mrs. Stratford and Miss Tremaine, and
to bring some music.

"What songs?" said Edith, quietly. Mrs. Blodgitt
ran over a list of half a dozen. "I don't know the
last," Edith remarked.

"Well, learn it, then! Be sure and learn it."

"Certainly," said Edith, "but my terms are high.
For an evening at your house I will charge one
hundred dollars. You had better get Patti."

Mrs. Blodgitt was confounded—Mrs. Stratford
amazed, but Florence laughed till the tears stood in
her eyes. Edith continued to look very quiet, and the

visitor, coloring till her face outvied the purplish crimson fuchsias in her bonnet, took her leave.

However, there were some few people who had both the courage and the inclination to cultivate the society of Mrs. Stratford's companion. One or two women were always civil to her, and two young men invariably made her an object of attention.

Edward Curtis, a frequent Lounger in Clara's boudoir, had the good taste to appreciate Miss Woodville, and Edith liked him vastly. He was strikingly handsome, with an almost feminine gentleness of manner, which contrasted most pleasingly with his tall and manly figure. It was easy to see that a sincere attachment existed between Clara and himself, but he was poor, and in marrying him, she must give up the luxuries of her fortune.

He appeared, Edith thought, unwilling to call upon her for this sacrifice, and she, doubtful whether it would be for her future happiness to make it. He was her constant attendant, and upon him had now settled all those suspicions and suggestions of which Mr. Stockton had spoken.

The other gentleman who showed himself alive to Edith's merits was one with whose attentions she could perfectly well have dispensed. He was of a vulgar style of beauty in her eyes, and displeased her sovereignly. She used to look like a great statue of snow when Mr. Julius Edlicott entered the drawing room in Fifth Avenue, and between Florence and herself there was sure to ensue a war, whenever the former rallied her upon her conquest of the ladykiller.

It was just before Christmas, and a dull gloomy day enough, that Edith, having got through her post-breakfast supervision of the hot-house flowers in the numerous vases, and the Spanish lesson, went to her own room to work upon a pair of slippers she was embroidering as a Christmas surprise for Florence. Deep in the mysteries of two stitches up and five down, she was startled by the sudden entrance of Léonide.

"How, Mademoiselle, are you not dressed?Oh my God, what shall we do? Now, if you hurry, maybe we have time to try another dress!"

"What's happening?" asked Edith, in Léonide's native French, raising her eyes to the waiting-woman, who stood in voluble astonishment before her morning-gown.

"But Mademoiselle, did you not know that Madame receives today? There is a crowd of gentlemen downstairs and Madame requests

Mademoiselle Woodville in haste. Mademoiselle, allow me to help you."

And all the while that Edith was hurriedly finessing her attire, Léonide kept up a buzz of remarks and suggestions.

"Miss Florence is beautiful, beautiful like an angel with her dress of blue brocade, and madame is ravishing; she wore her black satin trimmed dress. Miss Edith is always so simple, but it fits, so simple it is, she wears it with grace. Now Mademoiselle, see this here is ready," and Léonide, as she opened the door, murmured gently, "Mademoiselle is charming."

Edith found a large circle down stairs.

"I sent for you, my dear Edith," said Mrs. Stratford, "though Florence protested against it, insisting that if you wished to come, you would do so of your own accord. But here is a gentleman who vows you are under promise to him to sing "O mi Fernando" this morning."

"Miss Woodville cannot deny it," said Mr. Curtis, as Edith shook hands with him, and slightly bowed to the surrounding group.

"Won't any other time suit you?" inquired Edith in a low voice, as she took the seat he offered, besides his own.

"My dear," cried Florence, "he quotes the proverb in every known and unknown language, that 'a bird in the hand,' etc; and now that you have been disturbed from that mysteriously absorbing business which closes your door upon me everyday, you may as well gratify us."

The song was only half through, when a gentleman, who was about to be announced by the footman, perceived the listening group, and signing Thomas into silence, retired into the shadow of the folding doors.

Edith's voice was never more effective. Even Mrs. Brownfield listened, though she had an opera box, which by her own confession she only filled for fashion's sake, and never "minded" the singers.

"A thousand thanks," said Mr. Curtis.

"Beautifully sung," commended Mrs. Stratford with warmth, as Edith rose from the piano.

"May I not be allowed to add my meed of praise?" asked the gentleman, advancing into view.

"Frank!" exclaimed Mrs. Stratford, "how very glad I am to see you."

"Why when did you arrive?" said Florence, extending both her hands.

"Has your mother come?" inquired Mrs. Brownfield.

"How d'ye do?" said everybody else.

"Friends all," cried Mr. Frank, "I take it for granted that you are delighted to see me, and I am enraptured at seeing you. But before we go into any further exclamations or inquiries, pray, dearest Mrs. Stratford, present me," then, in a lower voice, "to yonder songstress."

"Most willingly. Miss Woodville, allow me to introduce to your notice and favor a gentleman for whom I entertain the highest regards, Mr. Francis Etheredge Millwood."

From the first moment of the stranger's entrance, Edith was struck by his likeness to her father, and a kind of vague suspicion crossed her, that this might be her cousin. When her doubts were solved, and when with a low bow and a profusion of courtly compliments Frank went through his presentation, it was too much for her. Rapidly through her mind the contrast forced itself.- The children of two brothers meeting as strangers. The one, happy, brilliant, dashing, carrying his handsome head with that proud air which spoke of a spirit never thwarted, surrounded by hands only too happy to press his own, and to hang upon his skirts; the other, proud too, but of that pride only which refuses to be trampled upon, poor, despised or unthought of, a hired companion, and yet beautiful and highly cultivated.

She returned her cousin's bow with freezing indifference, answered not one word, blushed violently, and then growing suddenly pale, fainted for the first time in her life.

Mrs. Stratford flew to support her, filled with alarm, and Florence grew almost as white as her friend. Mr. Curtis rang the bell. Léonide and Ann rushed in, armed with salts, hartshorn, camphor and aromatic vinegar. In a few moments Edith revived, heartily ashamed of her weakness, and in time to hear Mrs. Brownfield say to Miss Dolly Tennent, "Such a fuss over her! After all, she is only a kind of upper servant."

It was no comfort to see the fierce look which Frank gave the ingenuous lady.

"Thank heaven! Love," said Clara, "you are better now! Would you not prefer going up stairs? Florence will go with you." She gathered together Edith's long, beautiful hair, which had come undone, and tried to fasten it, but the massive braids fell again; so Edith twisted them up with her small white hands, and looking very lovely as she murmured something about "the oppressive heat," and a "headache," of course, left the room.

"Who, and what is she—besides being nearer perfect beauty than any thing I ever saw?" asked Frank Millwood.

Mrs. Stratford told the story she had got from Mr. Stockton, adding, "she has lived with me now more than two months, and really, when I look at her, and when I remember how reserved she is about her former life, and how isolated is her position, I begin gravely to tax my good friend Mr. Stockton with having imposed upon us some fairy princess in disguise."

"Yes," said Florence, who at that moment re-entered the drawing room, "we shall some day have her turn into dry leaves, or disappear through the ceiling, or suffer some such cruelty at her hands. She is quite well again, Aunt Clara, and insists upon my leaving her."

Mrs. Brownfield and Miss Tennent moved. They were anxious to say good morning and to go somewhere else, to relate what idiots the Stratfords were making of themselves about "that girl."

"Well, Frank," said Mrs. Stratford, after bowing out her guests, "this unlucky fainting of Edith's has prevented you from replying to any of our anxious inquiries. You seem quite puzzled about something."

"I *am* puzzled—I am trying to make out why your protégée's face appears so familiar to me. Oh, I have it! Do you recollect that full-length portrait of my grandmother Millwood which hangs in my mother's sitting room? It was taken just before the old lady's marriage. She was a great beauty, you know, in her day; now is not there a strong likeness between Miss Woodville and that picture? Miss Woodville's eyes are lighter, and her hair darker, and she has less color, but the peculiar cut of the eyebrows, and the shape of the face and chin are singularly alike."

"Bless me, Frank," said Mrs. Stratford, "you cling to your old habits! Still finding out resemblances! I thought that your last eminently unsuccessful one, when you assured Florence that her nose was precisely on the pattern of sister Margaret's, would have cured you."

"Yes, pray tell me," put it Florence, "how many frightful women have you seen at the South that reminded you of me?"

"Oh, ungratefuls!" said Frank, laughing, "I have a great mind to punish you for running an old friend in this way by refusing to give you the presents I brought from New Orleans, and by not telling you a piece of news which nearly concerns the world of

New York."

"Oh give and tell," said Florence.

"Don't bear malice," said Mr. Curtis.

"Well then, you must know, that the reason my father was so willing to go to Louisiana this autumn, a thing he detests, was because he was rather anxious to get out of *his* father's way; for by certain signs, known to him, it was plain that a storm would rage all the winter in the respectable household of the Millwoods."

"Why so?"

"Because—have you never heard that an uncle of mine ought to have married a certain niece of my grandmother's, and did not? She had an immense fortune, and my grandfather Millwood has never been reconciled to its slipping through his fingers. These cousins have, heretofore, lived very quietly. You know them, the Wm. Hamiltons? But this year they are to come out with an immense dash, and the old gentleman began to grow savage, from the moment that he heard of the *carte blanche* commission given in Paris for furniture, jewels, and dresses. So my prudent papa suggested to my meek mamma that as they had long thirsted for a sight of "our estates," they had better pack up the two girls, the governess, and themselves, and spend part of the winter in Louisiana. But the Hamiltons have been so long and so magnificent in their preparations, that they have just got into their rejuvenated establishment. Mr. Millwood is just at the height of his bilious indignation, and Mr. Frank Millwood is the only member of this dutiful family who dares return to face his angry fore-father."

"No one has heard of these grand doings," said William Barton, one of the still remaining gentleman.

"Of course not, my dear fellow. We don't tell everybody when we buy a new mirror, nor how much it costs, either. My great aunt, Mrs. Dunbar, the mother of Mrs. Hamilton, would never wear a gown, rather than have her whole circle of acquaintances know that it was bought at Stewart's or Beck's, and that she paid for is so many shillings per yard. They are a vastly high old crew that sail in the good ship Hamilton, and are so used to spending money, it neither strikes them with surprise nor do they fancy it will astonish their neighbors."

Frank was treading on delicate ground before a strictly New York audience, so Mrs. Stratford spoke:

"How does this effect us, Frank?"

"Why, for you ladies, there are to be balls without

number, and for the aspiring youths of Gotham there is an heiress to be won. For all this display, all this unwonted publicity, is to celebrate with fitting grandeur the coming out of Miss Hamilton, a young lady, who, by the death of two brothers, will be the sole enjoyer of that fortune my grandfather so coveted. If you desire it, Messieurs, I will put in a good word for any of you. Barton, she is desperately fond of waltzing, she writes me, but 'grandmamma objects.'"

"Oh, she writes to you, does she?" said Florence. "What does grandmamma say to that?"

"Grandmamma rather encourages it. The fact is, that no one has been more impressed by the glory of the Millwoods as set forth by Mr. Millwood of Millwood, than his sister-in-law, and she would be quite willing to take me under her tuition as one of her descendants. But Isabel objects, vows she will never marry a cousin, 'it would be so stupid to spend the latter half of one's life with a person whom one had seen all the former half,' and prefers something newer."

"Well, never mind, I shall take especial notice of Miss Isabel Hamilton, with a view to her turning some day into Mrs. Francis Millwood," said Mrs. Stratford, rising to wish good morning to the young

Busy Moments of an Idle Woman

men, who were going off.

"Wait, Curtis," said Frank. "I'll give you a lift. My carriage is at the door. You won't mind my coming in every day, will you, dear Mrs. Stratford? And you won't snub me always, Miss Tremaine? Goodbye. Make a thousand speeches for me to *la belle des belles*, that fairest of fair women. She is like my grandmother, smile as you may. You are not jealous, any of you?" He kissed Clara's hand, Florence poutingly refused him hers, and was off.

81

CHAPTER VII.

Edith pronounced herself quite well when the two ladies went to her room, immediately after their guests' departure. She had a cold, and she had over-walked herself the day before, that was all. But she still looked so feeble, and there were such deep lines around her mouth, and her hands and feet were so icy, that without her consent Clara covered her up on the sofa. Florence ordered her a cup of tea, and they both sat down to amuse her.

"You have made a conquest of Frank Millwood, Edith," said Mrs. Stratford, smiling.

"How do you like him, Edith?" said Florence.

"I did not speak to him. I scarcely noticed him."

"Did you not see that he was very handsome, with a manner rarely surpassed? He is so earnest under all his pleasantry; such a kind heart and sweet temper."

"He did not strike me particularly," said Edith coldly, and she began to talk about Mrs. Brownfield's new bonnet.

The next morning Miss Woodville had recovered her usual serenity, but showed no symptoms of admiration for Mr. Francis Millwood. He called early, wished to know their plans for the day, tried vainly to make Edith talk, and found her about as encouraging as an automaton that says "Yes" and "No;" she was not rude, but she doubled the veil of ice in which Mr. Julius Edlicott always found her wrapped.

"Is this beauty dull, or sulky?" whispered Frank to Florence.

"Neither," said Florence, firing up, "she does not like you, I suppose. She is very fastidious," she added archly, with a smile all coral and pearl.

Mr. Millwood was sorry that he did not suit the lady's taste, and ceased his attentions, but after a few days, he again felt himself irresistibly attracted towards the silent girl, with such great glorious eyes, and lips that would certainly say so much if they would only condescend to speak.

Mrs. Stratford complained to Mr. Stockton. "Do you know, sir," she said to him, the first Sunday after Frank's arrival, "do you know, that your ward can be very perseveringly insensible to the devotions of young gentlemen?"

"I hope so," replied Mr. Stockton, laughing, "or she will not be my ward long."

"Oh, but this is a peculiar case. Frank Millwood is not a great admirer. He wishes to be civil to Edith and she will not let him pick up her handkerchief or hand her a chair."

"Frank Millwood! Ah!" exclaimed Mr. Stockton, a little startled.

He looked at Edith. She returned the look with a slight elevation of her flexible eyebrows, and a forced smile.

"Oh, she will think better of it," remarked Mr. Stockton, "and not reject overtures."

"Never," exclaimed Edith, with the haughty air her face always wore when the Millwoods were in question. "I mean," she went on, "I wish attention from no fast young man of fashion. They do not suit my position," and she left the room.

"Do not press her," said her guardian,

thoughtfully, "let things take their course. Heaven guide them rightly."

On New Year's Day there was the usual delightful hurry, worry, and fatigue which accompany that important epoch. Edith was a mere spectator. She took no part in the reception of the ever-changing, never-ceasing stream of visitors.

Mrs. Stratford, in a dress of satin velouté of dark cerise, with massive gold and ruby-mounted jewelry, went through the ceremony with fortitude, and said "Happy New Year" and "A cold day" to each gentleman with unwearied sweetness.

Florence was in her element. She looked bewitchingly pretty in a blue silk with countless flounces, buttoned to the throat with large pearls, and her merry laugh sounded as inspiring as the sleigh bells outside.

Edith made no change in her usual costume, a bombazine covered with crape folds, but this sombre drapery was peculiarly becoming to her style, and strangers and elderly men who were rare visitors at Mrs. Stratford's went into raptures about her. Edward Curtis and she talked together for some time. He pointed out the notabilities, and gave a few quietly spicy anecdotes of some. Florence would rush up occasionally, beg Edith to emerge from her

corner and listen to her own praises, and bound off
again to welcome a new arrival. Mrs. Stratford sent
many a nod and smile from her side of the room,
and the morning Edith thought quite enjoyable,
when Mr. Curtis said:

"Here come Mr. Millwood and Frank. The old
gentleman never fails to pay a few visits, and this is
one of his houses. Frank takes him round at a gentle
pace, and then makes a dash to finish his own rather
longer list afterwards."

Edith for the first time was in the presence of her
grandfather. She examined him steadily. He was
tall, with straight, cold features, a determined
mouth, hair still quite dark, and a peculiarly neat
and English look.

He paid his compliments to Mrs. Stratford,
addressed a few stately words to Miss Tremaine,
and then his stern gray eyes rested upon Edith.

By this time Frank had made his way towards her,
only pausing to leave a box of bon-bons with Clara,
and one with Florence. "May I not offer you a
similar trifle?" he asked, deprecatingly, with a faint
color rising in his cheek.

He looked very handsome, and very captivating
under this little shade of embarrassment, as he held
out the pretty, fanciful package.

Edith's heart was steeled against his beauty, his perseverance, and his sugar-plums.

"I never eat bon-bons," she said, "thank you, they would be wasted on me."

"Oh, Edith!" cried Florence, running up, "they are not bon-bons alone. Look, Clara has a gold thimble with the daintiest carving, and her initials in diamond sparks, and mine has a flacon in the shape of an opal-eyed griffin. See what a love of a wretch! What have you?"

"Nothing," replied Edith; but Florence had taken the bon-bons from Frank, who stood in perplexed displeasure, and on opening the parcel, there lay an exquisite bracelet made of enameled heart's ease.

"Oh, Edith, how perfect!" exclaimed Florence.

"Edith!" repeated Mr. Millwood, from the distance. "Who is that lady, may I ask, madam?"

"She lives with me. An orphan, and almost friendless. Of her past history I know nothing, yet of her present excellence I can speak with delight."

"Ah," said superb Mr. Millwood, "a humble friend."

"Why not?" now came Florence's voice distinctly from the recess. Edith drew up her head haughtily, her eyes gave one flash, and then their full white lids slowly drooped over them, as she said with a manner that affected the deepest humility, and in a tone of the loftiest pride:

"I do not know why Mr. Millwood undertakes to offer me presents. A gift to an obscure stranger is either a charity or an impertinence; I am prepared to accept neither." She bowed with mocking grace and turned away. Florence silently replaced the trinket, and laid the strand on the table. Frank Millwood's face flushed with anger and mortification, and there was an uncomfortable pause.

"I beg Miss Woodville's pardon for my presumption, and need not assure her that this will be my last offense. I should have remembered that the date of our acquaintance can, indeed, be counted by days, and that during this short space, she has shown an unwillingness to know me better. When one feels within one's self a friendly sentiment, one can scarcely avoid supposing that it is mutual. My little offering, a string of pansies, seemed a permissible liberty on this day, and a gentle suggestion, that I hoped she would, at some time, think of me more kindly. I shall not cease to admire Miss Woodville's talents and beauty, but I shall no longer persecute her with my society nor my insolent offerings."

Frank concluded with a bow as profound as

Edith's had just been, and went back to Mrs. Stratford.

"Why are you so severe?" asked Mr. Curtis. "There is really nothing wrong in a New Year's gift, when made in this manner, and by a person who is on such intimate terms with your nearest friends."

"I am sorry you think me severe," replied Edith. "Mine is a difficult position. I cannot, I never shall act differently from what I have done today. Let us say no more about it. Who is the foreigner in the flashy waistcoat?"

But Edith was not as well pleased with her severity to her cousin as she ought to have been. There was something disarming, even to her morbid enmity, in the manly way in which Frank had spoken. She glanced towards him more than once. He was very grave, and his dark blue eyes retained their saddened, hurt expression. She could not but acknowledge that he was very prepossessing, and his notice of her was flattering. But then there came rushing over her the memory of her dead father, and she saw the prosperous, dignified Mr. Millwood, who seemed so little repentant of the past, so satisfied with himself, so proud of his grandson—so forgetful of his own lost child.

"Shall I got before all this crowd," thought Edith,

"and put him to shame? Tell him that his once favorite Albert died while painfully laboring for his bread? That his own granddaughter works for hers? No, indeed; there are not two people here who would not applaud his behavior. They would side with him, commend his *firmness*, and tell me to abide the consequences of my father's disobedience. And for myself, moreover, kindness from them would kill, not sustain me."

The thought of her idolized father brought two bright tears to her eyes; they would not be forced back, but rolled heavily down her cheek, so she turned to the window (being now alone, for Mr. Curtis had left her), and leaning her forehead against the cold glass, looked out upon the snow.

"Fairest Miss Woodville, are you learning your lesson?" said a voice she detested, Mr. Edlicott's. "Are you practicing to make yourself as dazzling and as cold as a snowdrift? But the sun brings a thaw to that. Will love never melt *your* heart?"

"I came here simply to be quiet," replied Edith, without looking towards him, "and trusted that the curtains concealed me."

"Nothing will ever conceal you from my eyes," said Mr. Edlicott, "and this will be as pleasant as a tête-à-tête. Why did you refuse to receive my note when I handed it to you in your book yesterday?"

"Merely, because having nothing to say to you, I have likewise no wish to hear what you have to say to me. Give me no more notes, or I shall be under the necessity of complaining to Mrs. Stratford."

"Why are you so cruel? Why will you not listen when I tell you how much I love you?"

"Perhaps you are not aware, Mr. Edlicott, that your engagement to Miss McIlvain is no longer a secret. You do not, I suppose, intend to forsake her for me."

"No, indeed, my dear creature. I am obliged to marry that girl, she is very rich, and desperately in love with me, but I confidently hope to devote my life to you, and to make those delicious lips learn to smile on me."

"Mr. Edlicott," said Edith, in a voice so fiercely calm that it even momentarily impressed him, "if you dare again to address me, in any way whatever, you will repent it. By the heaven above us! You shall know who I am!" And she swept past him through a side door to her own apartment.

It was time, for a burst of tears was near at hand. Did Edith think that she had been unnecessarily harsh to her kinsman? It is certain that after a few moments given to passionate indignation against

Mr. Edlicott and his insulting speech, her mind wandered to the rejected heart's ease. A vision of a pair of softly brilliant eyes, and a tender voice, modestly asking to have his bon-bons received, rose before her. She could almost have sketched from memory the outline of the face, with its dark chestnut mustache shading an admirably formed mouth, its high forehead, and its short, clustering, wavy hair.

"He is so like papa," she murmured, as her skillful fingers traced the features. Then she mused awhile, touched and retouched the pencil drawing, was about to tear it up, but sighing, changed her mind and placed it in her desk.

Frank kept his word. Almost every day he made his appearance at Mrs. Stratford's, but a bow to Edith on entering generally began and ended their interview.

There was no affectation in his manner. If she joined in the lively warfare always going on between Florence and himself, or put in a word when Clara spoke, he would reply with the deepest respect, and without hesitation, but he never addressed her first.

Edith was naturally so silent in company, that this coolness between her cousin and herself was not very noticeable, and after a while Clara and Florence seemed to forget the affair of the New Year's gift. Both ladies also were now plunged to the eyes in an exciting New York winter. Florence's head was filled with waltzes and polkas, bouquets and new dresses, a real live lord, and her usual train of admirers; while Mrs. Stratford more soberly (she was certainly grave for her age) thought a good deal of all these, but more still of her kind friend Edward Curtis. They used to have (Mr. Curtis and Clara) long, long talks in the little flower filled boudoir, and sometimes when these conferences were over, Clara would show traces of tears, and Mr. Curtis had a sorrowful resolution in his eyes, which made Florence often sigh. She said one day to Edith:

"Why do not things arrange themselves to suit us? And why are we all invariably acting so as to convey the least happiness to each other? How little it would take very often, it seems to me, to make such and such a person supremely blest, and yet that little is withheld by those who have it in their power to bestow it."

"Very true, no doubt," replied Edith, "to what do you allude particularly?"

"Have you not eyes to see, dear, that Mr. Curtis and Clara are excessively in love? And had it not been for this same spirit of contrariness, which I believe we all are cursed with, Mr. Stratford would never have made his detestable will, which prevents her from marrying. Now, what possible difference can it make to him, for his wife to be forced to remain single, if she has a mind to marry? Does any man dream that his widow, under these circumstances, regrets him?"

"Did I not hear Mr. Curtis speaking yesterday of moving to the West?"

"Yes, that is his latest notion. I don't know if he will carry out the idea. People talk so much about Clara and himself. I wish Mr. Stratford had been choked, or brought to his death in some uncomfortable manner, before he undertook to leave permanent Mrs. Stratford behind him."

"My dear Florence!" said Clara's gentle voice, as she noiselessly entered the room, "it grieves me to hear you speak so fiercely. Mr. Stratford's money was his own. I believe a great many excellent men have a posthumous jealousy of their possible successor. Besides, I shall always think that Mr. Stratford meant to alter his will—you know he did;" and Clara carried off the book of which she came in search.

"Dear me," exclaimed Florence, "I wish I were

half as good as my proper little aunt."

"Why does Mrs. Stratford think the will would have been altered?" asked Edith.

"Because, during his last illness, when she behaved like an angel to him, he said on some occasion, 'I have made a will that wrongs you, Clarry; I shall make a better.' After that, he was seen with a pen, looking over some papers, but when he died there was nothing found but the original will. His desk was picked to pieces all in vain. His brother, a Mr. Meredith Stratford, a disagreeable kind of man, who had been a good deal with him, and is now abroad, professed entire ignorance of any other documents. So we resigned ourselves to what we could not improve, being, in fact, rather glad that it was no worse. Lawrence Stratford was such a bear."

"Why did your aunt marry him?"

"Edith! What a stupid question! How many suitable marriages have you ever seen? I can count all those my few years have unveiled before me: two. One is a deaf man who has married a blind woman, and the other a couple of simpletons, who have not half an idea between them. Clara married him, because, I piously suppose, it was so ordained. Because this life, being a pilgrimage of penance and preparation, we are not permitted any wonderful degree of happiness. Those who marry are sure to think they might have have done better, and those who don't marry think just the same."

"I almost agree with you," said Edith, half smiling. "We hear every day, 'What a strange match!' 'What a singular match!' when Miss So-and-So marries Mr. This-or-That, two people apparently least made for each other. Whereas, 'the strange,' 'the singular,' is only justly described, when two persons of conformable tastes come together, it happens so rarely."

"Yes," said Florence, musingly, "every Jack has his Jill, but like carelessly-kept open-worked stockings, they are very apt to get mismatched in putting on. I wonder, Edith, where *our* Jacks are; and if they will ever 'turn up.'"

CHAPTER VIII.

The snow melted, it snowed again, again a thaw.
March came; then Lent, with its fasts (never kept).
Florence had danced herself quite thin. Now the
balls were over, jovial folk flew to Washington to
snatch a little more down from Pleasure's soft
wings, and there was a lull in New York. It was too
early to buy spring bonnets and mantles. Lawson
kept dark about the "fashions," Stewart's counters
were bare, "nothing new as yet, ma'am;" and Miss
Tremaine did not know how to pass the time.

"Let us go to Washington, Aunt Clara," she cried
out one morning, as they sat in the drawing room

with a knot of visitors—Mr. Curtis and Frank, of course, Augustus Woodbury and William Barton.

Edith was winding silks; she had before her a rosewood stand, on which she held her skeins, and was diligently disposing of hank after hank. Clara was working at the cover of a sofa cushion, and did about two stitches in every fifteen minutes. Edward Curtis had undertaken to sort her worsteds. Florence was idly lying back in a great chair, looking the very picture of a lazy little beauty. She had on a pink morning gown, with a little cap perched on the very summit of her saucy head, and surveyed the company with calm indifference.

"Let us go to Washington," she repeated, with the most *blasée* intonation.

The widow shook her head. "No, indeed, Florence, unless you provide me with a body guard of grenadiers to keep off the dreadful people one meets there. I would rather propose Charleston."

"Listen to the aristocrat! Clara the exclusive. She wishes grenadiers to hold snobs at bay, and she pines for the respectability of Charleston! When did you turn homeopathist, Mrs. Clara, and cure by an aggravation of the existing disease?"

"Come, come, Miss Tremaine," exclaimed Frank Millwood, whom a stray glance of Florence's had caught looking furtively at Edith, "Don't you know the Etheredges' hail from Charleston? It is a charming place, a capital place."

Yes, to come *from*," said Florence, "as I once heard a clever Charlestonian remark. It has an excellent name, and is best seen when you look at it over your shoulder. At this season too! Why, we should die."

"Is not yellow fever dangerous in Carolina?" asked Wm. Barton, with a really serious countenance.

"Always," said Florence, "particularly just now, when sparing the inhabitants it lies latent to pounce upon unwary voyagers. Mary Bronson wrote to me last spring from Charleston. She says the inhabitants only *live* during two months of the year, February (when they have the races) and May, when they walk on the battery. Now, Aunt Clara, we should neither hit 'the Race month' nor 'the Battery month,' so banish Carolina from your thoughts."

"Upon my word, Mary Bronson sets up for a wit! She must take her family by surprise," said Frank, laughing, and holding up a newspaper to shield his head from a shower of leaves, which Florence threatened to throw at him.

"Since you are such a sturdy admirer of the place,

Mr. Frank Millwood," said Florence, how does it happen that you never have been there yourself?"

"I never have had the time—I am kept so busy—my duties are so absorbing. But, seriously, if I were not going abroad this summer I should go to Charleston this spring."

"You are going to Europe, Frank?" said Mrs. Stratford.

"Yes, and I shall start early in the season, because I wish to go to Italy before those horrible fevers prevent me. Don't tell my revered grandfather, but I think it is time that some of us should go look after my Uncle Albert. Nothing has been heard of him for years."

"Is that beautiful wife of his alive?" asked Mr. Curtis. "I remember as a boy seeing her. She was a lovely creature."

"We have heard that she is dead; but my grandfather is so fierce about this branch of the family, and they have kept themselves so retired since Mr. Bradway's failure, that nothing is known, positively, about them. But I like all that I have ever heard of my Uncle Albert. And I don't admire him the less, because he married an unexceptional woman whom he loved, though by doing so he displeased his father. No man should stand in the way of his son's happiness, when the object of that son's attachment is irreproachable. He should not make his child the victim of his own private prejudice."

"Mr. Millwood," called out Edith's voice, in clearest, sweetest, and most liquid tone, while her large eyes, moist with emotion, turned upon him a look such as those eyes have never before given to living being—" Mr. Millwood, will you assist me here?" Frank sprang to her side, coloring with pleasure. Edith placed in his hand the end of her tangled skein. "I admire an honest sentiment honestly expressed," she said, and then tremblingly arranging the silk, she relieved him from the easy task, and held out her own perfect little hand. Frank silently took it and bowed. Edith seemed about to speak, then changed her mind, and, according to her usual custom when betrayed into feeling, left the room.

"What a curious *dame de compagnie* Miss Woodville is," remarked Augustus Woodbury. "I thought such people knew their places, and never spoke unless spoken to, and had no airs, and were not better than governesses."

"There are different creatures of every species," said Miss Tremaine, "Some companions may be what you describe, and others are like Miss Woodville. Just as among young men about town, some are like you, and some are like Mr. Frank Millwood."

Augustus almost understood. He barely gazed the meaning, however, but got up, saying, "I have such a bad cold in my head, I must go home, I feel so stupid."

"You are subject to colds, are you not?" inquired Florence, with a gravely sympathizing look. "What a very tiresome person Mr. Woodbury is," she exclaimed, as the door shut him out. "He ought to marry, to have someone help him along with his load of dullness."

"Do you think Miss Woodville is indisposed?" murmured Frank to Florence.

"No," answered Mrs. Stratford, who had caught the words, "but I am inclined to believe that our peerless Edith has one fault: she is capricious—she is--"

"Oh, Aunt Clara," cried Florence, "not capricious! She is difficult to please, but let her once be satisfied with a person, and she is unchangeable. You need not look so intensely happy," she whispered to Frank, with a mischievous laugh.

CHAPTER IX.

"What o'clock is it, Florence?" asked Edith, as she and Miss Tremaine turned to walk up Broadway one afternoon.

"Just four," replied Florence, looking at her tiny watch, which sparkled among the charms at her waist.

"Oh, then, I shall have quite time enough. I wish very much to see Mr. Stockton. He dines at half-past four, and will probably be at home now. You do not mind going back alone? I shall pay him my visit and be with you again before our dinner hour."

"Very well. Don't stay, or someone will carry you

off as you flit along through the twilight. *Au revoir."*

The girls lightly nodded to each other, Florence pursued her way, and Edith went down Ninth Street.

Mr. Stockton was delighted to see her. She sat down with him to dinner, and chatted while he disposed of his soup and fish. When the roast appeared she got up.

"Now, sir, I must leave you. It will be growing dark, and Mrs. Stratford will have a thousand terrifying fancies. Come early on Sunday."

"Wait, my dear, and I will take you back."

"No, indeed. It is a pleasant walk now, and I shall be at home in time to change my dress." She kissed her guardian, and stepped out into the street.

Drawing her cloak warmly about her, Edith was crossing Broadway when a little girl, just in front, frightened by the rapid approach of an omnibus, instead of making haste, stood irresolute, till the horses were nearly upon her.

Edith, with impassive feeling, started forward, snatched the child towards her, and felt as she did so the breath of the "off" horse upon her shoulder. It was a narrow escape, and she was thankful when, unhurt, they both landed upon the right side of Broadway again.

The little girl was excessively alarmed still. She shook violently, and tears were in her eyes. She was a nice-looking little thing, humbly dressed, but clean and tidy.

"Where do you live?" asked Edith, patting her head kindly. "You are too young to be sent out alone in these wide streets."

"I live just across there," answered the child, pointing to the Fourth Avenue, "is it not far, but-"

"But what?" inquired Edith.

"Couldn't you, please ma'am, cross that street with me? I am so afraid," and she looked imploringly in Edith's face.

Edith did not fancy going into the Bowery, particularly as it was getting late, but the child had such pretty eyes she could not refuse her. Taking her hand, she retraced her steps, and conveyed her charge over the dangerous street.

"There is Mother looking out for me," said the little girl, pointing to an open door, where stood a middle-aged woman. "Thank you a great deal, ma'am."

"I will speak to your mother," said Edith, "she ought not to send you out, or let you go out, until you can take better care of yourself."

"Mother! Mother!" cried the child, "I was almost

killed by one of those big carriages, and this lady helped me."

The little story was soon told. The woman was deeply grateful. She called her husband, who was busy unpacking a box, to inform him of the risk they had run.

"God bless you, ma'am," said the man, respectfully. "It would have been a dreadful thing! Maggie said she knew the house where we sent her, and would be very careful, and was not afraid. My name is Williams, ma'am. If ever you should stand in need of anything I can do, call upon me. I am a gardener by trade. I hope to get established here again, and when I have flowers, tell me where I can find you, to bring you a bunch sometimes."

"My name is Miss Woodville," said Edith, pleased with the appearance and manners of her new acquaintances, "and I live at Mrs. Stratford's, No.——Fifth Avenue. I shall be glad to hear that you are doing well, and pray keep my little friend Maggie out of Broadway."

"Stratford!" repeated the man. "Any relation to Mr. Meredith Stratford? Is she a pretty lady, with brown eyes, and a bright color in her cheeks?"

"Yes," said Edith, "she is his sister-in-law."

"And did the gentleman die, ma'am?"

"What gentleman?" asked Edith.

"A sick gentleman that I signed a paper for."

Edith started. "Tell me about that," she exclaimed.

"Oh, it is not much," said Williams. "I used to have a garden on the Bloomingdale Road. A small affair, and Mr. Meredith Stratford used to get bouquets from me. One day, he met me on the street and told me to bring some flowers to Bleecker Street the next morning, about eleven o'clock. He gave me the number, and I went there and asked for him. While I was waiting in the passage way, the pretty lady with the brown eyes came out from the parlor, smelt the flowers, and asked me who they were for. I said as how they had been ordered by Mr. Stratford, and she looked puzzled, and then the servant came back and said, Mr. Meredith Stratford would come to me in a minute. So the lady nodded her head, and said, 'Oh, my brother,' and went away."

"Well," said Edith. By this time she had walked into the house and sat down in a chair the woman offered, and little Maggie leant upon her knee, while the man stood up before her.

"Well ma'am, Mr. Stratford came downstairs and looked around, and there was no one in the hall, and he told me I might bring the flowers myself up stairs, for the gentleman they were for would get me to do a little job for him. So I followed him up and into a bedroom, and there was a sick gentleman sitting up in an armchair, with some papers beside him, and he said that the flowers were very sweet. 'I am much obliged to you, Meredith,' and then he said to me, 'My good fellow, you can sign your name?' I told him I reckoned I could, so he gave me a paper and I put my name to it, Isaac Williams, and he offered me a dollar, and said, 'That was all.' But I was not used to such things, so when Mr. Stratford took me downstairs, I told him I hoped there was no trouble coming to me for singing my name. He laughed, and said 'No, indeed, I would have taken up the man servant to sign the paper, but the gentleman does not like them to talk about it in the house." I have never heard any more about it to this day."

"Did you ever see Mr. Meredith Stratford again?"

"Oh, yes. He used to get bouquets often, and then it was he that sent me to the West."

"Ah!"

"Yes, ma'am. He meant it kindly. He had a grant of land out in Michigan, and thought it would make my fortune. And so I sold out my garden, and moved West. He let me have the tract for next to nothing, but the place wa'n't healthy, and two of our children died," the woman wiped her eyes as he said this, "so we thought we would just come back to the old trade. Planting corn ain't like growing flowers, but we have been away a matter of four years. That's why our Maggie, who has been so long in the backwoods, can't keep her head from the horses' heels."

"Have you been to look for Mr. Stratford?" said Edith.

"Why, no, ma'am," said Williams, hesitating. "The fact is, Mr. Stratford said, 'Don't come after me, Williams, if you ever come back, for I shall have no opinion of you. A man who can't get on in a new country like that proves that he ain't worth for anything.' So I haven't been to see Mr. Stratford, because, I suppose, he would think me mighty good for nothing. Is he well, ma'am?"

"He is in Europe," said Edith, very calmly, but a thousand thoughts were passing through her mind. She remembered what Florence had told her. She remembered Mrs. Stratford's conviction that her husband had made another will. She remembered the character she had heard of Meredith Stratford, a hard, disagreeable man. He was sole heir, after the wife's death or marriage, to his brother's fortune. Florence had said that he professed to know nothing of any paper. Could the document that Williams signed have been the new will? It was a bold and hazardous stroke. Could Meredith Stratford have destroyed it?

Edith's first decision was to see Mr. Stockton.

"Goodbye," she said, "you will not move from this house immediately?"

"No, ma'am, we rent these rooms for a month to come."

"Then I shall see you again."

She stooped to kiss Maggie, and almost ran to her Guardian's.

"Mr. Stockton is just gone, Miss Edith," said Jane.

Edith was sadly disappointed. She scribbled three lines. "Pray come to me, dear Guardy, early tomorrow morning. Don't fail. It is important."

"Let him see that as soon as he returns tonight," she charged Jane.

It was now so late that Edith stopped an omnibus, determining to ride home. She drew down her veil, and sat very quietly in the nearest corner, scarcely perceiving who were her neighbors, so busy was her mind with the discovery of what might prove such future happiness to her dear Mrs. Stratford.

"I knew it must be you. Who else moves with the grace of Miss Woodville?" said Mr. Edlicott's voice. He was beside her.

Edith had not seen him since New Year's day, but her mind was too much occupied to have room for indignation. She merely looked at him, and then turned away. But Julius was not to be so daunted. There were only two other people in the omnibus, a man and his wife apparently, sitting at the further end, so that he thought he had it all to himself.

"I have wished to explain to you," he began, edging closer. Edith touched the check string, handed up her sixpence, and jumped out.

It was so quickly done, that Mr. Edlicott could not pay his fare fast enough to follow immediately on her footsteps, but he saw the flow of her black skirt and made after it, just in time to see her take a gentleman's arm, and hear her say-

"I saw you from an omnibus, Mr. Millwood. Was I wrong in thinking that you will give me your escort home?"

The formidable Julius did not stop to put in his claim to that honor. He brushed past, and vilifying his luck, soon hailed another omnibus.

Frank was very much surprised, but he knew

Edith too well to worry her with questions, or to overpower her with assurances of protection. He began to talk about Mrs. Stratford and Florence. Then in her own good time Edith explained that she had been detained while intending to pay a short visit to Mr. Stockton; that as it was growing late she took refuge in an omnibus, from which the threatened insolence of a person had driven her.

"What person?" demanded Frank.

"You surely do not suppose that I would tell you his name, even if I knew it?"

Edith's heart felt so light this evening, that her manner was unusually kind. Her voice was not so cold. There was a ringing sound in it, and a more familiar tone. Frank was thrown off his guard. He had determined never to go a step father than Miss Woodville advanced. He would not again suffer a rebuff at her hands. He had taken no advantage of her flattering speech a week or two before, and though they seemed a shade more friendly, still it had appeared, after all, but a tepid sort of regard on her part. Now she leaned on him almost confidingly, and her bewildering eyes sent such thrills through Frank Millwood's breast, that prudence, in vain, set her seal upon his lips.

"Am I taking you out of your way?" Edith

inquired.

"No. I would like to ask Miss Tremaine if she rides tomorrow morning. Do you never ride, Miss Woodville?"

"I am a great coward on horseback. I do not ride well."

"Let us teach you. I should be so happy to give you all the instruction in my power, and Miss Tremaine is a capital equestrian. I will not be fierce with you, or expect wonders at first. You shall never be forced into daring feats."

"You are very kind," said Edith. "You have always been kind and attentive to me," she continued with hesitation, "and I know that I have been ungracious. I have wished several times, lately, to tell you so, and to say that," her sweet melodious voice trembled a little, "that my temper is faulty, and—and—"

"Say no more, dear Miss Woodville," interrupted Frank softly, while his heart beat in a transport of delight. "You cannot guess how such words enchant me. Oh, that you would be always so kind! Surely you must long since have seen that I am made happy or miserable just as you treat me."

One quick feeling of pleasure shot through Edith. She could scarcely account for it, but in a second, the strong prejudice of her life was triumphant.

"Mr. Millwood," she said gravely, almost haughtily, "if you are amusing yourself at the expense of a humble friend of your friends, pray let me assure you, that your words are understood. If you would have me take them literally, allow me to decline the honorable pinnacle on which you would place me. Edith Woodville can have no part in the life of Mr. Francis Etheredge Millwood."

"I cannot think that you believe me capable of so dishonorable a thing as to amuse myself as you suggest. It is only your 'pride that mocks humility,' Miss Woodville, and the first reason influences the last. I am in earnest. I will not be put aside in this way. My love for you began, I know not when, I think it was the very first moment I saw you. Do you think you can never give me the faintest return?"

Edith stopped. They were in the Fifth Avenue, and nearly at Mrs. Stratford's door. She fixed her eyes earnestly on her companion.

"Between you and me there is an impassable barrier. It never can be overthrown."

"A barrier," repeated Frank, "of what kind? Since when?"

"It existed before we met. This is all that I can

say. Even this is too much," replied Edith, hastily.

The remembrance of certain boyish follies crossed Frank's mind. He had made himself rather conspicuous two years before by an absurd passion for a little dancing girl. Could Edith mean this? There was a slight blush and tremor about her, and as she resumed her walk she kept her face turned from him. "Surely she is not so very prudish?" thought Frank. "Does she expect to find a man who has been perfect all his life?"

Then came a second idea. "Is her heart no longer in her own keeping? Was I too late in meeting her? Does she love someone else?"

Frank did not think he was justifiable like the heroes of novels in putting the question, but he risked the first doubt.

"Then you would tell me, Miss Woodville, that I must abandon hope? That I must see you, love you, and be silent, though I have never *loved* any one else?"

"You have known me three months. Do you fancy that you will think of me always? I am an obscure, insignificant woman, whom you have generously invested with qualities that, probably, I do not possess. Your path lies in the full light of day— mine through the shadiest alleys. Would you break your grandfather's heart by a second *mésalliance*? I have heard people speak of Albert Millwood; while his story is remembered I shall never give a thought to you. Better as it is. Marry your cousin, Isabel, and forget that I live. Do not imagine that I fly to be pursued. Goodbye. Respect my forlorn and almost friendless state. Believe me deeply grateful for your honorable preference, but hear me swear, that so surely as I bear the name of Woodville, I cannot, will not encourage any tenderer sentiment."

"I am answered," said Frank; "you shall be safe from my persecutions." A bitter smile played around his lips. "Mercenary!" he said to himself. "She thinks my family would treat me as they did my uncle, and the very idea prevents any feeling on her part."

They were at home. The footman threw back the door with emphasis. "Mrs. Stratford and Miss Tremaine have been very anxious, ma'am. John went round to Mr. Stockton's for you, and came back saying that you had left."

"Oh, Edith!" cried both ladies, running out. "Where have you been?"

"Frank was with you," said Mrs. Stratford. "I am glad of that."

Florence looked from one to the other. She pursed

up her pretty lips, shook her head knowingly, and signed to Frank to follow her.

"You have offered yourself," she whispered, as they entered the drawing room.

"Yes, and been refused," said Frank. "Some one has talked to her about my Uncle Albert, and Miss Woodville evidently loves gold, and as evidently wishes to run no chance of losing a real, positive establishment. Her beauty and talents she counts upon to secure a fortune in possession, not an heirship in expectancy. The Millwood estates have already been settled upon one child to the exclusion of another."

"For shame," exclaimed Florence. "Look at Edith! That creature, whose every gesture and whose every word speaks character of the highest order! Would she refuse to listen to the voice of her heart, because the man she loved *might* forfeit his inheritance in marrying her? Will she marry for an establishment, when she prefers to be a hired companion, and to be sneered at as an inferior, rather than live with her guardian, upon whom she has no legal claim?"

"I tell you, she herself mentioned my uncle, alluded to his disinheritance, and told me that it formed an impassable barrier between us."

"You misunderstood her. And as nothing else will convince you, I will tell you something which happened yesterday, and which, I think, is a better solution of the mystery. For mysterious, of course, it is, that Miss Edith Woodville should not be ready to snatch with eagerness the proffered hand of Mr. Francis Millwood."

"You are jeering me," said Frank, sadly. "I was not such a coxcomb as to be sure that Miss Woodville would, with pleasure, listen to my suit. But, at the same time, I must confess that I thought I had some chance of success, that she would promise to learn to love me. And besides," here Frank drew up his handsome head, haughtily, "she might have considered it, instead of requesting me not to pursue her."

"Suppose she is in love with someone else?" suggested Florence, softly.

Frank caught her hand.

"What do you mean?"

"It may be wrong to tell you what I had no right to see, but yesterday morning I went into Edith's room. Her desk was open, and I thought she was writing. As she did not hear me, I went up, laid my hand on her shoulder, and my eyes involuntarily discovered that it was no letter, but a pencil sketch of a man, that lay before her. She hurriedly threw it in her desk, blushed violently, a very unusual thing for her to do, and asked, with a little pettishness in her tone, why I walked so lightly, that I had startled her."

"Did you know the face?"

"I did not even see it. As you may suppose, I made no remark about it. Edith soon recovered her usual equanimity; only a greater tenderness in her voice during the rest of the day, seemed to ask my pardon for her momentary anger."

"I am much obliged to you, Frank," said Mrs. Stratford, entering, "for bringing back my stray lamb. She says she had an adventure. A child was almost run over, she took it home, and then after trying an omnibus ride, preferred calling upon your services. Stay and dine with us, unless you are afraid of the over-roasted meats."

"Thank you," replied Frank, "I have dined already. The one gentleman invited me to his early repast today. Good evening."

He hurriedly went off. He quickly returned. "My compliments to Miss Woodville," he said.

"Oh, she begged me to renew her thanks to you. She is dressing."

"Ah me!" sighed Florence.

"Sighing! Florence darling," exclaimed Mrs. Stratford. "What flower is faded? What ribbon crushed?"

"I have been thinking over a love story. That little fellow Cupid appears to have quarreled definitively with Hymen. They no longer hunt in couples."

Clara sighed too.

CHAPTER X.

"So, my dear Edith, you think that you have made a discovery, and that this man Williams is honest and tells the truth?" said Mr. Stockton.

"Indeed I do, Guardy. What is your opinion?"

"We must first speak to Mrs. Stratford. I hate to give her false hopes, but this may prove—I only say *may*, my sanguine Edith—of vast importance to her."

Edit flew to bring Mrs. Stratford. Miss Tremaine was with her.

"May I not come too?" asked Florence.

"Oh yes, I suppose so."

"What is it all? You and Mr. Stockton have been closeted like a couple of Vehmgerichter."

There was no jesting when Edith retold her tale. Clara perfectly remembered the man with the flowers, whom she saw in the hall. But then the paper he witnessed might be some lease, some bond, some trifle. "And Meredith Stratford! Could he have destroyed the will? Impossible!" But even while she urged her doubts, there was a growing brilliancy in Clara's eyes. She embraced Edith again and again. "Dear Edith," she said, "you are a living blessing. How much I may yet owe to you?"

There was no time to linger. Mrs. Stockton went to find Mr. Stratford's lawyer. Williams was brought up, rather alarmed, as he was a timid kind of man, but he told the same straight story. He could prove that Mr. Meredith Stratford had sent him to the West. Close researches did not bring to light any deed bearing Williams's name. Letters were written to Mr. Meredith Stratford; from Mr. Stockton, informing him of the impending suit; from his own lawyer, asking if he could produce the paper which Williams witnessed.

Of course, this was not the work of a day, and gradually the secret (as such things invariably do) leaked out.

The widow was more popular than ever, especially with young men and with mammas who had sons to dispose of.

Florence's opinions on the subject were variable. Sometimes she would wake up in a fever of joy, she was so sure of success.

"She had always thought Meredith Stratford a Blue Beard, Richard the Third kind of creature, who, for want of heads to chop off, took as *lesser evil* any stupid, dreary vice, or crime;" and she would nearly begin to congratulate Edward Curtis, until Clara's blushes stopped her. Then the next day, all was wrong.

"To be ugly, stiff, and stingy was common enough; but to burn or otherwise make away with a will was not a thing done every day." Meredith Stratford might be bad company, but she was very much afraid he did not deserve hanging. Alas! It was far more natural that her deceased uncle (by law) had cajoled Clara with talk about another will, while he chuckled inwardly at her credulity.

Clara herself said very little. She was even more quiet than usual, and spent a great deal of time in her own room.

So speeded by the spring, and people began to arrange their summer plans. One letter had arrived from Mr. Stratford. He could not remember much about Williams, thought he was a man whom he recollected befriending. His brother had a great many business papers always to be witnessed; different persons had signed for him. They might find Williams's name somewhere. He (Mr. Stratford) was going to the East. There was not much use in writing to him again on the subject. No doubt, his brother's widow wished to marry, and this fable was got up by some pretender to her hand. There was no use in bullying him. He had the law on his side.

To this epistle was returned the answer that Mrs. Stratford would set apart from her yearly income so many thousands as her lawyers would deem necessary to defray the expenses of the suit, and that, if it lasted for ten years, she would not cease trying to make good on her claim.

Whether Mr. Stratford was really an Oriental traveller, and the mails across the desert failed, or whether he travelled *à la Dumas*—only in the imagination—and invented it as a ruse to linger the proceedings, no one knew, for he lived very obscurely abroad.

Matters stood on this uncertain footing when our party moved to Newport for the summer. It was a

very jovial season at this pleasant place, and
independent of hotel amusements, there were
innumerable cottages filled by agreeable owners
and lessees. The Hamiltons had established
themselves handsomely, gave weekly dances, and
the heiress was to be seen everywhere. The John
Millwoods had ventured from their plantation, and,
with Mr. Millwood, had followed the popular
movement. Frank had not gone to Europe; he had
put off his departure till the autumn, and gossip said
that he was engaged to his cousin Isabel.

A watering-place life will not permit seclusion, as
Edith soon discovered. People have a way of
popping in at all hours; and then an accomplished
musician like Miss Woodville, whose voice and
execution will be heard through open windows,
could not always refuse to let herself be listened to.
There was an energetic, tremendous kind of woman
at Newport, who with a lion's share of enthusiasm
and cleverness, and no public object upon which
legitimately to exhaust its outpourings, was
constantly forming musical parties in the intervals
between her fights with everybody. She came down
upon Edith with a force, a vigor, a passion perfectly
surprising. She over-powered her by the vehemence
and fluency of her address, and carried her off for

an immediate practicing, bonneted and shawled, before Edith had made up her mind to accept the complimentary position of prima donna in Mrs. Jerry Ponsonby's hardly worked and much kept under amateur opera troupe.

Nobody dared object to Edith's supremacy, if Mrs. Ponsonby so willed it. The former "first lady," a rather high-spirited woman, whom her family treated with prudent respect, pouted a little, but so long as she stood beneath the lash of Mrs. Ponsonby's tongue, and the glitter of her bright eye, when that delicate white hand pointed to the notes of another score, Julia Munroe meekly obeyed, and learnt to perform "second fiddle."

"Miss Woodville is an angel!" cried Mrs. Ponsonby, haranguing her regiment. "She is worth all of you put together. Jerry, give Miss Woodville a chair. Mr. Ponsonby, my dear! He would be a good-looking man if it were not for that dreadful Ponsonby nose; but you must not waste time on him now. Sing that for me."

Edith described the scene when she came home, and sent Florence into convulsions of laughter. But she confessed that her own stout heart had trembled, and that she meant to reserve her "readings of Mrs. Ponsonby" for a very select circle.

This piratical abduction, of course, drew Edith very much before the exciting Newport world. In spite of herself she was now included in most of the merry-makings.

She had never before seen Frank Millwood, decidedly, "in company." She was amazed at the petting, the spoiling, the devotion he met with on all sides. He was the leader in every party and his word was the fiat of fate. Any lady would throw over any other partner when Frank Millwood invited her.

"Yes, I wonder his head is not turned by all this nonsense," said Florence, when Edith spoke of it, "but he takes it with a calm air, very much as you receive compliments, Miss Edith."

Isabel Hamilton was very attentive to my heroine. She used to drive her out in a wagon, drawn by a pair of spirited horses, which it took both of the heiress's little hands to hold in. She talked a great deal of Frank, praised him very much, loved him very much, and seemed not in the least sentimental about him. Frank always treated her with kindness and brotherly care, but one day Edith's temper was ruffled. She perceived on Bella's plump, round arm, a bracelet of enameled heart's ease. It must have been the recollection of the impertinence she had suffered in having it offered to herself, for that "simple string of pansies," worn by Miss Hamilton, annoyed her exceedingly.

They were driving, and Edith's eyes constantly glanced towards her companion's left arm.

"Oh you are noticing my birthday present. I was eighteen yesterday, and when Frank heard it, he rushed off and brought me this pretty bracelet. Don't you remember. I was at Mrs. Stratford's, and we had just been talking of Augustus Woodbury's constant attention to Julia Munroe, and you said, you wondered how any man could continue devoting himself to a woman when she found his society distasteful to her. Then I remarked that, anyway, she was too young to marry, for she was just of my age, and I was eighteen that day."

"I do not recollect," said Edith, faintly.

"Oh yes, and I observed, moreover, that if he were really in love, Julia ought not to make him ridiculous, for there is something touching in being the object of a sincere attachment. Then you said, "No! A love that is not desired should be crushed at once." On our way home, Frank was very grave. He said, on taking leave, 'You are not a beauty, Bella, but you have a kind little heart,' and in the evening he sent me this bracelet. It has an inscription," continued Isabel, smiling. "Whoa! Lighting, whoa!

Flash, quiet, sir." She drew in her horses, and loosed the bracelet; within was engraved, "To her who would *give* heart's ease."

"Very pretty," said Edith, "extremely pretty. Let me clasp it for you again."

Miss Hamilton had never found Mrs. Stratford's beautiful friend so silent as on this delicious afternoon. Being a cheerful, merry little thing, it rather bored her, but she chatted away good-humoredly for both, and then, the drive over, deposited Miss Woodville at the cottage gate.

"Send the wagon home, Bell, by your groom, and spend the evening with us," cried Florence, running out. "There is all sorts of news, Edith. Aunt Margaret has written that I have been away from Ravenswood quite long enough. She seems to have forgotten the visit of three weeks and five days I paid her in April."

"But she does not wish you to come back now?"

"Indeed she does, but Clara is as firm as a 'limpet to the rock,' and intends to keep me. Then Mr. Stockton sends a short note to say he will be here tomorrow."

"How good that is of him," exclaimed Edith, "the sight of his kind face will make us all hopeful and jovial."

"Then I wish he were here this evening, for your friend, the Autocrat, has issued a ukase, signed Catherine Ponsonby, announcing that she will take tea with her 'dearest Mrs. Stratford,' at 8 o'clock. The very presence of that strong-minded creature terrifies me into silence."

Miss Hamilton and Edith laughed.

"I shall certainly stay now," said Bella, tossing her reins to the groom and springing lightly down. "To see you lost in taciturn surprise, Florence, will be worth witnessing. My love, Evans, to mamma, and tell her I shall take tea here, and ask Mr. Frank Millwood to come for me."

Mr. Stockton's note was hurriedly written. Both Clara and Edith thought something decisive had taken place in the will business, but Florence was in one of her downcast and despairing moods.

"No, indeed, nothing favorable has come to pass, I am very sure. Perhaps Williams has turned out to be an impostor!"

Punctually at 8 o'clock, Mrs. Ponsonby appeared. She was accompanied by her husband, and by a young gentleman whom she presented as M. Jules de Versac.

"He is not wife hunting, Miss Hamilton, so you need not run home," she whispered to Bella.

"Charming tenor voice," to Edith, and to Mrs. Stratford she vouchsafed the intelligence that he had brought her letters, was the son of an Englishwoman, and perfectly safe. To Florence, Mrs. Ponsonby never spoke; she considered her an empty-headed little flirt.

M. de Versac conversed in his mother's tongue admirably, and was really a very handsome and agreeable youth. He singled out Miss Tremaine as his object, almost immediately, so that Florence failed to act up to the promised role, by which she had induced Bell Hamilton to remain.

"I never dreamed that one of Mrs. Ponsonby's protégés would interest me, or vice versâ. How disgusted she looks!" said Florence, in a low voice to Edith, as they gathered around the tea table.

Mrs. Ponsonby liked to take her evening meal at the Stratford cottage. Clara's housekeeper provided bountifully and well. The coffee was always clear, the tea strong, the cakes fresh, the sweetmeats luscious. Very often a *pâté de foie* tempted the company after a long drive or walk, and little dainty dishes of cold viands met invariably a hearty welcome from Mrs. Ponsonby.

On this occasion, there were certain delicate squares of pastry filled with a compound which amazingly struck the fancy of the guests. Mrs. Ponsonby was the first to taste them.

"Jerry," she exclaimed, after the third mouthful. "Jerry, try these. A new sensation! Eat one."

"They are made by Miss Woodville," said Clara. "Would you suspect that she is a capital cook? This is her receipt, and they are never good unless Edith superintends them."

Mrs. Ponsonby rose. She took Edith's hand, solemnly. "I always knew that you were a glorious creature," she said, "but to find you a good cook, places you now on an eminence unattainable by any one else. I have a nephew; he is as clever as any man, and as good as any woman. Won't you be my niece?"

"She cannot answer till her guardian arrives," said Mr. Curtis, entering and taking his place at the table. Amid the general laugh, Frank Millwood, who was following close behind him, handed, unobserved, some flowers to his cousin Isabel, which she blushingly received.

But there was one person who saw the maneuver. Edith watched them both with jealous attention.

"I never knew you to eat cream and sliced ham together before," murmured Florence, archly, to her friend.

Edith started, and pushed aside the plate on which she had, really, unconsciously spread some ham with cream.

"They say that there were tableaux, last night, got up at the 'Ocean,'" said Mr. Curtis.

"That was the reason, therefore, of Mrs. Fields's violent attempt to carry you off, Frank, from our house," said Bella.

"Certainly," replied Frank. "Mrs. Fields was grand. I heard all about it this afternoon. In each tableau, and I believe she acted in all of them, her costume got thinner and less. At her third appearance some prudish ladies retired."

"It was very select, however," suggested M. de Versac. "They took the largest private parlor and made a frame of the bedroom door opening to it. The effect was not very good, because the audience was too near. But if the perspective failed, the bare shoulders were all the prettier, the blue veins on them were countable by the farthest off man."

"Did you act at all?" asked Florence.

"Oh no, I had just got here, but I have the honor of Mrs. Fields's acquaintance, so she let me in, and we smoked cigars after the performance."

"Why not get up a well-conducted tableaux in this house, Mrs. Stratford?" inquired Mrs.

Ponsonby.

"I am willing, if you will undertake the management." The idea was caught at immediately; the ways and means were discussed; a meeting arranged for the next day, "at lunch time," amended Mrs. Ponsonby; and with a little music, and a great deal of talking, the evening closed in great harmony.

CHAPTER XI.

Long before lunch time came Mr. Stockton. He had news, and it was news worth bringing. Mr. Meredith Stratford had written again: he had consented to give his attention to this absurd business, and he hinted a compromise.

"I should not like," he wrote, magnanimously, and Mr. Stockton, of course, had brought a copy of the epistle. "I should not like to drag my brother's name into court, to give his reasons for making his wife remain his widow; and I should not like to have my word set against the word of a gardener. Fortune to me is a matter of indifference;

competence is all I ask. Mrs. Stratford believes that my brother changed his mind about the disposal of his property. I know that he was tender-hearted and madly attached to his wife. Her tears may have melted his purpose. He may have consented to allow his money to pass into hands which were inimical to himself, (I make no assertion, I do not say that my brother felt he could point to his successor), but I only protest that I am aware of no such intention on his part. I confess that his body servant, Peter, was with me one day at his bedside, when he requested me to take measures for the alteration of his will, but nothing came of it. However, as I may be mistaken, as my brother was but mortal, he may have relented, and as I would pay as much respect to his half-uttered wish as I would to the most formally signed and sealed legal document—bearing his name—I can only suggest that had he made another will, he would, probably, have left me a present income adequate to my position as his nearest relative and bosom friend. Five thousand per annum would have been a suitable and proper sum."

This extract gives a faint idea of this wonderful document, which filled Clara with delight. She was indifferent to Mr. Meredith Stratford's hint about her husband's successor. She very nearly joined in Florence's peals of laughter at the deceased gentleman's "tender heart" and "mad attachment," and she authorized he lawyer to offer, instantly, the five thousand per annum, if the defendant would execute a deed, conveying to her the undisputed right to the twenty-five thousand of income remaining.

"You would spoil all with your haste, my dear lady," said Mr. Stockton. "We need not show this deceptive rascal that we have never ceased trembling for our success, by the haste with which we accept his modest conditions. After all, we should find it very difficult to make good our claims if he were to hold out. But the wish to avoid a long suit and the likelihood of your outliving him, and *perhaps*, the prickings of a torpid conscience have brought him to this proposition. He thinks that it may be as well to spend five thousand every year from this moment as to starve on a very scanty revenue— he has not more than nine hundred a year —till he is too old to enjoy your thirty thousand, even supposing that you die first. But five thousand a year is not a sum picked up every day. We must answer that, sure of success, or even indifferent to the result, you do not choose to divest yourself so large a slice from your pin money. Hold back a little, and he will press on. By the next steamer he will give directions to his lawyers to draw up the deed and hand it over to us at once, if we will consent to pay, without further negotiation, four thousand, or some such reduction."

"And suppose he should die meanwhile? Or change his mind? And trust to my going off with a chest complaint, or a falling in love," said Mrs. Stratford, smiling.

"Suppose, when we accepted breathlessly, he should reconsider and decide to await the trail, since we appear so eager to get rid of nearly one hundred thousand dollars? Patience, patience, dear Mrs. Stratford. I can now *almost* confidently say '*Hope.*' Turn your thoughts, if possible, to something else. Edith and Miss Tremaine must brighten you up. How do you find Newport, my dear child?"

They all began to talk of the tableaux. Mrs. Ponsonby's name made Mr. Stockton smile. He evidently was acquainted with the fervid style she indulged in.

"Put yourself in her hands, madam. That is right. I defy you to think of wills, courts, or brothers-in-law, if Catharine O'Brien fixes her attention upon you and yours. From the time she was fourteen, she has considered the world not her 'oyster,' but her piece of putty, which she could twist, shape, cut and fashion to suit her own white fingers. Good Lord! Here she comes, Jerry following with piles of engravings. My blessing be upon you, fair ladies," and Mr. Stockton rushed through an opposite door.

The preparations for the tableaux went on swimmingly. Mrs. Ponsonby was not one "to let the grass grow under feet," nor to waste her time in consulting, discussing, arranging, and deciding. She fixed the day at a fortnight's distance, so as to allow for any accident or detention. She would not hear of first asking people to perform, and then suiting them to pictures. "No, indeed, choose the pictures, and then find men and women who *may* represent them." She had no hesitation in her decisions. A capital memory, a good store of prints, and an artistic taste enabled her to make a list of very pretty scenes, and of persons to fill them. No one disagreed with her, so that her spirits were excellent, her temper unruffled, and her society delightful.

She made bon-mots enough to have freighted ——'s Magazine for a twelvemonth, and grew so gracious that Florence was really afraid that she might speak to her.

In the afternoon, Mrs. Stratford and Edith drove around with her to invite the actors and actresses. They enjoyed, excessively, Mrs. Ponsonby's manner and mode of treating the fine ladies, who were determined to accept, but who thought it elegant to begin by declining. Woe to her who played this game! She, at once was caught in her own trap.

"Oh, very well," Mrs. Ponsonby would say, "take it or leave it, but make up your mind at once. Fortunately, Newport is not Sahara, nor the Dismal Swamp. Somebody else lives here. We shall be glad to have you, but don't force your inclinations."

A very, very few she condescended to coax. Edith, for instance, who pleaded her mourning, and stood out bravely against the terrible publicity, but everybody was against her, even Mr. Stockton; so she yielded, and agreed to look her best as the statue of Hermione in a "Winter's Tale."

Alas! Mrs. Ponsonby did not always use her influence and her soft accents in so natural a cause. There were dull and insignificant-looking people whom she was heard sucking up to, quite as warmly, for, as there are specks on the sun, there were breaks in Mrs. Ponsonby's independence. She did not stand firmly against the lordly encroachment of *very* rich or very fashionable people who chose to oppose her. The stiff knees of her will bent sometimes, but she made up the balance by fiercer demonstrations to yielding subjects, so soon as she came across a victim, after her bestowal of smiles and congees upon the Pompelinos, and the Brian Boru Thompsons.

Every day there were rehearsals. Carpenters were at work, upholsterers came from New York, dressmakers were imported from the surrounding country, pastry cooks had *carte blanche* to furnish a supper of incalculable expense, and the hotels, far from thinning off at this advanced season, became more and more crowded. The news of the expected fête had spread abroad, and everybody hoped for an invitation.

Mrs. Stratford was almost alarmed, but Mrs. Ponsonby took the whole thing off her hands.

She bullied the performer corps, she wrote the directions to tradesmen, she ordered the costumes, she commanded up props from all quarters, she ate dinner at the house everyday, and she made Jerry direct the cards to the envelopes.

Mr. Stockton had gone back to New York, but was to return for the important affair.

"I cannot tell you," wrote Edith to him, "how brilliant Mrs. Ponsonby! She comes out stronger

each day, and her energy is perfectly wonderful. I
never tire of listening to her sparkling speeches,
when she is in a good humor, and I never cease to
be amazed at her powers for *work*! I cannot repeat
to you any thing that she says, for her words lose
their greatest charm when you divest them of the
fire, passion, and earnestness in which her voice
clothes them."

CHAPTER XII.

At length came the eventful day. All was in readiness. From the best performer down to the curtain drawer, each man and woman was perfect in his or her part.

Mr. Stockton had been permitted to witness the last dress rehearsal, which he had arrived in time to see, and he pronounced them the very perfection of tableaux medium.

Before the first guest at night, came Mrs. Ponsonby arrayed in "living scarlet." Busy, self-concentrated, yet with an eye to all, like a general on the eve of a great battle who sees his troops well appointed, eager for the fight, and making a grand array, but who fears some trifling inaccuracy may turn a glorious victory into a shameful defeat.

She made her "*corps*" line up before her. There was not a petticoat, nor a toga, a Marie Stuart cap, nor a Turkish turban which she did not scrutinize with grave deliberation. Happily there was a commendation for all, but for two people there was praise.

Edith and Frank Millwood especially delighted her.

"She is exquisite," Mrs. Ponsonby whispered to Frank, "and you both look wonderfully well this evening. I am not surprised that you prefer this grand creature to your cousin. Though Miss Hamilton is very pretty, more pretty than necessary, for an heiress, and really a creditable girl, still, to my mind, Edith Woodville is something rare."

"You are very kind to give me credit for such good taste," replied Frank, trying to smile, "but from what do you divine my admiration?"

"Pooh, pooh! Don't by missy-ish. You can't help it. I see it in your look, in your voice, every time those great eyes of hers lift their heavy, straight fringe towards you."

"But that is so seldom."

"Oftener than you would have me believe."

"She tries not to see me, when I am present."

"Then she makes up for it when you are absent, for I saw a pencil sketch of you in her desk yesterday, when I went to hunt up a sheet of paper."

"Of me? Dear Mrs. Ponsonby," cried Frank. "You mistake."

"Dear Mrs. Ponsonby never mistakes what her eyes show her plainly. I can't talk to you any longer. See those women daring to sit down! They will crush their dresses out of every decent fold." and she made a rush at two unfortunate girls, who were destined to play standing-up characters.

"Strange, mysterious Edith," thought Frank Millwood. "When will she give me the clue to her unaccountable behavior? Since that evening when I made such an ass of myself, I have constantly fancied that I could read in her eyes, or in her tone, a meaning which her words invariably deny. What is she after? What would she have me do?"

"Star-gazing, Frank?" asked Mrs. Stratford's voice, "Mrs. Ponsonby is calling for you."

Clara was not, of course, to appear in the tableaux. She left the "green room," to receive her guests at the entrance door of her pretty drawing rooms, which soon were crowded.

I do not intend minutely to describe these tableaux. Like love scenes, every one has their own reminiscences, which are brighter and fresher than any thing my pen could paint. Necessarily there were some more beautiful than others, but all were equally well got up, and perfectly enacted.

There was a "Game of Life," in which Frank Millwood was the "Youth," a certain dark-browed, genius-faced Mr. Lawrence, the "Mephistopheles," and Isabel Hamilton, the "Good Angel," which elicited unbounded applause.

People chose to see a peculiar meaning in the great tenderness of Isabel's attitude, and remarked that it was not her usual expression of countenance. It was only because Mrs. Ponsonby had divined in the lines of Bell's face the capability for such a look, and had so arranged her drapery and her large wings as to etherealize the ordinary mere prettiness of the heiress.

Florence was "Roxalana," refusing the flattering visit proposed by the sultan, in Marmontel's pretty tale. The Oriental surroundings, the grave Messinger and the lively Frenchwoman, were admirably depicted. You could fancy from Florence's air, what a volley of sparkling impertinences were issuing from her saucy, red lips.

A little foot was tossed mischievously into view, as if she had just thrust it out to prove, "I have no dust on my feet, and I do not drink tea so early."

Between each representation a band of music filled up the pauses and prevented weariness on the part of the audience. And as Mrs. Ponsonby had decided that each person should perform only once, there was no delay for a change of dress, and the pictures, therefore, succeeded each other with agreeable quickness.

Edith's tableau was in Mrs. Ponsonby's opinion the most artistic, and she reserved it as a suitable conclusion, to be dwelt upon the longest.

"Hermione," clothed in her snow white robes, was the most exquisite personation of the living statue. True, the text was not strictly followed, for the admiring Leontes (Mr. Curtis) could scarcely now have said—

"But yet, Paulina, Hermione was not so much wrinkled, nothing so aged, as this seems."

The attentive "group" were very secondary objects, and plaudits long and loud convinced Mrs. Ponsonby that she had judged her labors aright. Some elderlies present went back to the days of Mrs. Siddons, and protested, that even she had never more beautifully nor more impressively rendered this celebrated scene.

Loud calls were made for "the Manager" when the curtain fell, and amid cries of approbation and gentle clappings of hands, Mrs. Ponsonby stepped forward, and bowed, as if overcome by the gracious approval of her admiring friends.

But a waltz drew away attention, and the lookers-on were just as well pleased to become themselves active performers, and to go through their own little roles.

The united wishes of Mr. Stockton, Clara, and Florence, had finally persuaded Edith not to resume her black dress that evening.

"Just to gratify me, consent to wear a white one, no matter how simple," they had each said.

So Edith yielded, and laying aside her veil and short-waisted drapery, made her appearance in a white crape perfectly unadorned, but admirably adapted to her pure skin. She looked younger, and more suited to the excited scene.

"Why, Edith, you have on a ring!" exclaimed Florence, "see here, Bell, is not this pretty?"

Edith was putting on her gloves as they were leaving Florence's bedroom, where Miss Hamilton had gone to give a more comfortable inspection to her appearance, than she could do in the general dressing room.

"It is very pretty," said Bell.

Edith took it off. "I don't know why I have put it on," she said.

At that moment Mrs. Stratford called her, and she ran down stairs leaving the ring in Bella's hand.

It was an old fashioned, but quaint piece. Two clasped hands held up a jeweled flower, of which the leaves were arranged to spell Regard, with the initials of each gem. The stones were of a good size, and beneath them a little braid of hair was concealed.

"I will give it back to Miss Woodville in the ballroom," said Isabel to Florence, as they went down.

The whole Millwood family had turned out on this occasion. Mrs. Dunbar was on the arm of her brother-in-law, Mr. Millwood. Mr. and Mrs. Hamilton had thought their Isabel's tableau more beautiful than any other. Mr. and Mrs. John Millwood were wondering to themselves if Frank would not now see that Isabel was quite as charming as that Miss Woodville, whom he had several times informed them was considered "very lovely."

The two little Millwood girls, of whom the elder

was sixteen, though not yet out, had been permitted to come, to see their brother and cousin perform.

The waltz was at its height. Augustus Woodbury was spinning Julia Munroe as if his name were Herr Von Spingalen, his vocation to whirl, and she the wonderful tumbler kept upright on his arm. Mrs. Ponsonby seemed daring the dancers (even James Roberts) to upset her, or to order her away, as she stood bringing down her words like sledge-hammers (for she was talking earnestly right in their path), and Florence had already gone off with her partner.

Isabel dutifully went to receive her parent's praises, and kept twisting on her finger Edith's ring, while Mr. Barton was petitioning her for a turn.

"What ring is that, Bella?" inquired Mrs. Hamilton.

"It belongs to Miss Woodville," answered Isabel. "Is it not fanciful?" and she gave it to her mother. Mrs. Hamilton looked at it, at first carelessly, then a surprised expression crossed her gentle face.

"Whose did you say? Mamma!" she called to Mrs. Dunbar, then stopped, and over her smooth but matronly brow, a stream of color swept.

"Can you bring Miss Woodville here?" she asked her daughter. "No, stay, dear, I will go to her." Mrs.

Hamilton was very much agitated. Isabel felt quite nervous, she caught her father's arm, and they followed down the room.

Edith was talking to Mr. Stockton, Mrs. Stratford was listening to her, and Frank Millwood stood near. Straight up to her walked quiet Mrs. Hamilton, who seldom spoke to any one.

"Will it be an impertinence to ask you, Miss Woodville, how you came by this ring?"

Edith hesitated. She really knew no more than that it had been her mother's—one of the very few trinkets which they kept after their misfortunes. But a vague notion of some approaching event made her silent and almost confused.

"Speak, my dear Edith," said Mrs. Stratford, "what is the matter?"

"It was my mother's," answered Edith, firmly, at last.

Mrs. Hamilton seized her hand.

"I see the likeness now," she cried, "of which Frank Millwood has spoken. Was you mother Ellen Bradway?"

"She was," said Mr. Stockton, gravely advancing.

"My cousin Albert's child!" exclaimed "fair Alice Dunbar;" and she folded close to her heart the shrinking girl, who felt stunned by the sudden discovery.

"This ring was mine," said Mrs. Hamilton. "I gave it to my cousin for his bride. This braid of hair is mine."

The whole affair had passed as quickly as we read it, but not, of course, unobserved. Murmurs went around. No one had heard distinctly, yet all guessed that something important had happened.

"Mrs. Hamilton has fainted," said somebody.

"No! Miss Woodville has taken a ring of Mrs. Hamilton's," said somebody else.

Up came Mrs. Dunbar and Mr. Millwood. Mrs. Hamilton's eyes, filled with tears, turned upon them.

"Oh, sir!" she cried, looking up to her uncle, "this is Albert's daughter."

Mr. Millwood drew back.

"I know no such person. No such person lives for me."

"He lives for no one," said Edith, and her haughty tone rivaled her grandfather's. "He sleeps in his humble grave. There let him rest."

"Do you not acknowledge you son's child, sir, now that accident has betrayed a secret she would have starved rather than tell?" said Mr. Stockton.

Mr. Millwood paused irresolute.

"Come to me, Edith," exclaimed Mrs. Hamilton, the tears raining down her cheeks. "My cousin Albert was very dear to me. His daughter shall be my daughter. Are you willing, Isabel?"

"Alice!" cried Mrs. Dunbar, frowning.

Isabel moved beside her newfound relative and kissed her.

"Clear away this genteel mob, or let us go into another room, my dear lady," whispered Mr. Stockton. "Edith will die among these people. Old Millwood is killing her already."

The supper room door was close at hand.

"Let us go in here," said Mrs. Stratford.

Mrs. Hamilton, when she found herself alone with her own family, Mr. Stockton and Clara, gave free course to her grief and joy. She still held Edith's hand.

"Frank told me of the stranger so like my aunt Millwood. And your deep mourning was for my cousin?"

"Calm yourself, my dear Alice," said Mr. Hamilton, a man as reserved as his wife generally was. "Edith shall live with us; she shall not suffer from her grandfather's resentment." And he, too, kissed the pale brow of the poor orphan, who had not for so many months heard the names now bandied about.

All her precautions had been in vain. She was known—and except by this branch of her father's family, by the woman he had unavoidably slighted —she was looked upon with dislike and suspicion.

There was no occasion for exercising that stern self-denial, that refusal of the Millwoods' proffered good offices, which she used to fancy that she was magnanimously declining!

And Frank! Where was he?

She sat silent, still, beneath this unexpected blow.

"I shall recover presently," she thought.

The door opened: John Millwood, his wife, and daughters, followed Mr. Millwood into the room.

"My niece Edith," said John, "my father has changed his mind. He is here, ready to take you beneath his roof, and to consider you as his grandchild."

"His charity I do not need," said Edith, proudly. "For any kind feeling you may bear me, sir," she tuned to her grandfather, "I thank you. Here is my guardian. He was my father's only friend."

Frank had stolen up behind her. It was to his urgent and decided words that Edith was indebted for this tardy recognition.

"Was this 'the impassable barrier," Edith?" he

murmured.

"It was, and it exists still," she replied.

"Tut! Nonsense," said Mr. Stockton; "my child, you may be as romantic as you choose, but when your grandfather consents to receive you, do not reject the offer. I do not yet understand how he has been brought round, though I think Mr. Frank Millwood can tell us."

Mr. Stockton's hint was correct.

Frank had threatened that if his cousin was not immediately taken to their hearts, he would leave the country forever.

"I could not stand the shame that will fall upon us from every honest man. Here is a young girl who has never injured any of us; who has never made herself known to us; who has scorned to ask bread of us. Who is beautiful and clever beyond her most beautiful and clever associates, whose reputation, temper, and principles are admirable. And we sit by to see her work as a hired companion, or as a governess, because her father displeased my grandfather. *We* would suffer, sir," he continued to John Millwood; "for by this act of disinheriting our fortune grows, and calumny would not hesitate to say that we counseled the act."

Moved by this reasoning and by Frank's threats,

John Millwood urged his niece's claims likewise, and Mr. Millwood, having made up his mind to such generous forgetfulness of his strong past resolutions, proceeded to put them into effect. Moreover, it must be confessed, that Edith's beauty and grand air had impressed her grandfather, and it contributed not a little to his relenting when he considered how well she would do the honors of Millwood. How handsome she would look entering a ballroom or how "Young New York" would gather around this first-water brilliant, in its now gold setting. They would bow down before this spotless lily, now that, storm passed, it would raise its pure head upon its emerald-green stalk, and be proclaimed queen among the flowers!

Edith's prompt refusal to be acknowledged by him, fanned into brighter glow the feeble flame of his grand-paternal affection.

Like some family despots, he rather admired, sometimes, a sturdy opposition, when it did not arise among his lawful subjects. He liked to succeed, in spite of obstacles, so that it was with a softening manner that he said,

"I commend your independence, Edith, and your gratitude to Mr. Stockton, who has befriended you, but now your position is changed. You are Miss

Millwood of Millwood. I shall endeavor to forget your father's disobedience, and trust that no like ingratitude, on your part, will reward me for my care and kindness."

Edith stood unmoved. She was about to repeat her refusal with additional bitterness, but Mr. Stockton and Clara stopped her.

It is needless to set down the arguments and reasoning they whispered during this awkward pause.

"I counted upon this denouement," Mr. Stockton wound up, "when first I placed you with Mrs. Stratford. Submit yourself to your grandfather. My poor friend, Albert, longed and hoped for this day. I will show you his last letter, where he says, "Do not thrust my Edith upon them; but if they seek her, tell her to forget their unkindness to me, which rankles in her loving heart, and to be reconciled.'"

The die was cast. Edith gave her hand to her guardian, and he led her slowly up to her cold, sever grandfather.

"I resign my charge, sir. I give into your keeping a good daughter, a noble heart, a lovely woman."

Mr. Millwood drew Edith's arm within his own. "I accept her, sir, and thank you for your hospitality to my granddaughter."

It was a curious scene, and made as unlifelike a tableau as any that Mrs. Ponsonby had singled out for representation that evening.

"Shall we return to the ballroom?" asked Mr. Millwood, bowing low to his hostess.

Edith, who had remained pale, as grave and immovable as if turned into stone, now signified her wish to retire.

"By no means," said Mr. Millwood, "you may as well be seen at once. I am not ashamed of you," and a courtly smile curved his lips.

This worldly old man felt no pang at the loss of his son, but he was already proud of that son's child.

Mr. Curtis had been requested by Mrs. Stratford to "keep the ball in motion" during her absence from the rooms, and the party consequently found the festivities proceeding with accustomed spirit and animation. But Edith's entrance produced a buzz—a sensation, and many inquiries.

"All the Millwoods in riot! What does it mean?"

"Miss Woodville on Mr. Millwood's arm!"

"Mrs. Hamilton wiping her eyes!"

Then came Mr. Millwood's dignified, sonorous tone, as he presented Edith to his nearest and most distinguished friends.

"My granddaughter, Miss Millwood. The only

child of my son Albert."

The company understood. The father had been disinherited, the daughter had lived incognito.

Edith longed to get away, to weep; to think of her father; to escape from these curious eyes; to get reconciled in the solitude of her own chamber to her new life; to learn to feel kindly to those whom she had taught herself to hate!

But my heroine was, after all, a girl of eighteen. Gradually her brow relaxed from its unbending sadness. There was something amusing, if there was not something gratifying, in the sweet flatteries now offered to her. How the people pressed up to make their compliments. The "brilliant" was set, the "lily" had reared its proud head. Edith's court was formed, and her grandfather was enchanted.

Alas! Aristocratic Mr. Millwood had a taint of vulgarity in his well-born composition: he enjoyed public demonstrations.

After a while Edith managed to slip off. She wished, at least, to go and talk to those who had always loved her and always been proud of her.

"Edith!" Frank whispered, stopping her, "my cousin Edith, may I hope now?"

She gave him one look, and, with half a smile, turned to Isabel, who left Frank's arm to join her.

The girls ran down the steps into the little garden, where the moonlight lay soft and dreamy.

"And you are my own dear cousin," said Isabel, caressingly, "How strange! And if I had not carried off that ring we would never have known it. Why did you conceal yourself from us? Mamma, papa, and I would have taken care of you. I am sure I am quite willing to give you half my fortune now, I am so tired of hearing of my heiresship. I begin to think that it is all that I possess worthy of notice, and I should be glad to find myself reduced to my individual level."

Edith laughed-

"Suppose I call upon you now, dear Bell, to give me something that you value. Will you do it?"

"Willingly, name it."

"Your bracelet of heart's ease!" said Edith, watching her narrowly.

"Ah!" cried Isabel, clapping her little hands joyously, "I was right, and Florence was wrong. Certainly you shall have the bracelet, provided you will take the donor too, and not make my darling Frank miserable any longer."

Edith protested and blushed in vain. Bella clasped the heart's ease on her cousin's arm, and it was evident that Florence had told the story of the New

Year's Gift.

LETTER FROM MISS TREMAINE TO MISS
MANVERS.

New York, November 17th, 18——.

MY DEAR AUNT MARGARET:- I promised to
give you a minute account of Edith's wedding,
which, by the way, she never ceased regretting you
were not there to grace. Your headache could not
have come more inopportunely, for it was a grand
spectacle, and a most interesting occasion.

Mr. Millwood had decided that nothing should be
wanting on his part, to mark his admiration for, and
pride in, this newly-found descendant.

I say "admiration," advisedly, for I think the old
gentleman is not getting much farther than
"admiration" for anybody, and I fancy he stands a
little in awe of Edith. She treats him with profound
respect, but her love for her father was so holy, so
absorbing, and so entire, that she cannot think any
devotion to herself can cancel past neglect of him.
She appears likewise to have identified herself with
her mother, and to feel that it was through love for
them that her father suffered. Altogether she has
romantic notions about her duty to her parents, quite
different from the stately reverence she pays to her

grandfather. But this kind of behavior seems to suit Mr. Millwood's taste, and fond as he used to be of Frank's more affectionate attentions, it is easy to perceive, that now, Edith's grave, but constant *civilities* please him more. In fact, people say that his short-lived objections to his grandchildren's marriage arose more from the idea of Frank's not being worthy of Edith's alliance, than from his old notion of wishing through Frank to get possession of the Dunbar fortune, now resting on Isabel's head.

The ceremony took place at twelve o'clock, and the reception was from one till three. Bella, Mary Millwood (Mrs. John's eldest daughter), and I were the only bridesmaids. Edith gave us our gloves, pink silk dresses, and to each a complete trimming of old point lace. Her own dress was extravagantly rich, from the beauty of depth of her *point d'Alençon* flounces, which Mr. Millwood had imported with an unlimited order. She wore pearls valued at twenty thousand dollars (New York style now, to name the price), and you can, perhaps, if you exhaust your recollections of beautiful women, imagine how very beautiful she was. The bridegroom was by no means thrown into the shade, however, he was handsomer even than usual.

Presents have been showered upon Edith. There

were great salvers groaning under a weight of plates and countless bracelets, necklaces, and trinkets. Connections of the Millwoods and Etheredges continued to pour in their gifts till the last moment. I could not help wondering if the money which half of these gorgeous gewgaws cost would have been given to that sorrowful man who died in Warren Street eighteen months ago, or to that pale girl in black, who taught at Mrs. Callender's school.

But these are not recollections to bring up now. The bride and groom went that afternoon to Hilton, on the North River, which is the next place to Millwood, and was purchased by Mr. Millwood from Mr. Bradway when the latter failed. It is the former home of Edith's poor mother, and at this season too, will, I think, be but a melancholy spot for a honeymoon. But Edith wished it, and her word is the word which rules.

They will return in time for Aunt Clara's nuptials, of which the final arrangements are nearly at an end. That wretch, Meredith Stratford, has been forced into positive action, and Mr. Stockton hopes to place the necessary deed in Clara's hands in a fortnight. She and Mr. Curtis are so happy. At Edith's wedding, yesterday, Mrs. Ponsonby said, "It makes me ill to see so many perfectly-contented

people, and to think that I shall never be able to
look as you do, till I have, at least, a thousand a year
added to my income, and of which, now, I don't see
the slightest prospect."

Envious scandalmongers who cannot appreciate
the delicacy of Edward Curtis's conduct, say, "It is
evident what was his attraction—the fortune." But
we who know him, can think with pleasure of his
disinterested determination to devote his life to her,
but never to persuade her to such a sacrifice.

Goodbye, my dear Aunt Margaret. I shall be with
you as soon as Clara can spare me, but absent or
present, lively in New York or quiet at Ravenswood,
I am equally your affectionate
FLORENCE.

P.S.— There is a young Frenchman whose mother
was a Miss Manvers, M. Jules de Versac, who
wonders if you are related. I shall present him to
you before long.

OLD MAIDISM
VERSUS MARRIAGE

PART I.

Seven fair girls! What a pretty sight! All young, all lovely, and all sufficiently clever to make their carefree gossip entertaining.

It was a cold winter evening during the Christmas holidays, and the well-warmed room with its huge crackling fire of great oak logs, its deep crimson curtains, its old-fashioned yet comfortable chairs, its luxurious sofas piled with cushions, and its general air of sturdy hospitality, would have formed a delicious contrast to gladden anyone hardy enough to venture out into the dismal, dark night, and then, shuddering, return to this cozy apartment. It was the dining room of Mrs. Bloomfield, a rich widow, who, with her one son and only daughter, was "keeping Christmas" at her fine old estate, Oak Forest.

Dinner was just over. The brilliant light of numerous candles in tall silver candelabra shone upon the relics of the dessert, where hastily were displayed walnuts, pecans, West India fruits, liqueurs, excellent old Southern Madeira, ground-nut paste, and other articles, foreign and indigenous. The whole spread was richly served in beautiful glasses, massive plates and gorgeous china, all of some fifty years' date or more. At the head of the table sat Caroline Bloomfield. She had taken the seat just quitted by her mother, and, with her fairy fingers, was stripping the thick yellow peel from a golden banana. Just eighteen, above the usual height, fully and gracefully formed, with raven hair and dark blue eyes, regular yet expressive features, and a manner by turns soft and winning, dignified and reserved. Caroline was likely to long retain the reputation she had already acquired of an accomplished coquette, for there lurked a spark of charismatic mischief in her bright eye. She had a way of sweeping her cheek with the fringes of her white lids before she slowly raised them that was

infinitely startling to an unaccustomed observer.
Then her complexion was pure and dazzlingly fair,
and her black braided tresses, falling low upon
either side of her oval face, were, at the back of her
small head, gathered into a richer plait that crowned
her queenly brow with a natural tiara.

Next to Caroline sat her most intimate friend,
Laura Stanley, a quiet, grave woman of twenty, with
no very great beauty of face or figure, but handsome
nevertheless from her air of intelligence, fashion
and elegance. She was exquisitely dressed, as usual,
and, bending over a newspaper, she was the most
silent of the party, only occasionally looking up
with a smile when some lively witticism from the
group attracted her notice.

Her younger sister Fanny, a giddy little sixteen
year old pet, had left the table, and was lounging on
a sofa. Fanny's golden ringlets tossed back upon the
cushion that supported her head, her brilliant hazel
eyes half closed, her red, pouting lips opening but to
yawn, and with her tiny foot stretched out and
buried in the long hair of Bruno, Caroline's
Newfoundland dog, her entire person wore an air of
languor very seldom visible in this prettiest of pretty
creatures.

Adelaide Clifton was diligently shelling and

eating nuts. She was the musician of the party, a fine-looking, handsome girl, more like a Northern belle than Southern. She was slight, slender and active, with a bright color, and was more striking than delicate in her appearance.

A soft, gentle maiden, with great blue eyes, luxuriant fair hair, a lovely figure, a sweet, yielding smile, and rather sentimental altogether, was at Caroline Bloomfield's other side. Louise Merrington was a general favorite.

Very slight and fairy-like, with auburn hair and black eyes, snowy skin, and such a mischievous mouth, was Louise's cousin, Julia Merrington, who formed the sixth of this bevy of beauties.

Seventh and last, but with the exception of their young hostess, the handsomest of all, was Annie Hamilton. She was a glorious brunette, and it would have been almost impossible at the first glance to find a fault in the perfect picture she presented of youth and beauty. But a closer examination showed that, in a certain nameless grace, she must yield to Caroline. Such was the collection of Charleston's fairest daughters, who might have challenged criticism. But where were the cavaliers that should have been in attendance upon this bright phalanx? Let us listen to the young hostess:

"Well, really, I had no idea we would miss those men so much! Very tiresome of them to choose this evening to pay their visit to Colonel Hunscome. I told George, the Colonel had a dinner today, and would be sure to keep them till late tonight, but dine they would at two o'clock, and off to Briarly. So we must suffer the ennui of a 'ladies' party,' with nobody to tease and abuse."

"Worse than that, Carry," said Adelaide Clifton, "the night is growing so dark and dismal, that if they attempt to return, they may pitch into some of the swamps, and we will be forced to really mourn. For my part, if harm comes to Willie Lawrence, I shall put on weeds, for I consider myself 'as good as engaged' to that gentle and genteel Adonis, don't I, Fanny?"

"I neither know nor care," said pretty Fanny, almost roused into a toss of her languid head, for her flirtation with Willie Lawrence had often been broken in upon by Adelaide's persistence in calling upon the handsome youth to attend to her and her musical affairs.

"Don't make Fanny wretched, pray," laughed Caroline, "can't you see the poor child is suffering now? She is thinking of Mary Hunscome's attractions, and shows her misery by going to sleep.

Dear Fan, don't gape your head off, for though we have often heard Madame G. say 'that child has no head—'"

"Now, Caroline, don't you try to be as witty as Annie Hamilton, it's a signal failure. You neither move me, nor succeed in your effort at brilliancy. Lie quiet, Bruno. Aren't these women too stupid?"

"Thanks, Fanny," joined in Annie Hamilton, "for the compliment to me, and, as I am bound, after that, to subscribe to all your sentiments, I do say, I think we are very dull. Since Mrs. Bloomfield went off just now to read that long letter, we have done nothing but grumble, except Laura, who pores over that "Saturday Courier" as if it were the philosopher's stone of amusement. I, for one, will give my silver étui to any young lady of the present company who will devise some entertainment for us to pass the time, till these recreant knights return to us and to their duty."

"What candid young souls we are! What amiable simplicity pervades our group!" said Julie Merrington. "How unblushingly we proclaim that we can't amuse ourselves for one evening with the 'Lords of Creation,' apropos, sing it, Addy, will that pass the time, and gain me the étui, hey, Annie?"

"No, I forbid music," cried Annie; "Adelaide

walks over us at all times, with her skill, execution, taste, voice, knowledge, and, besides, don't you see she has been devouring nuts for the first time these three weeks? She won't be able to sing decently, and, as there is no one to profit by our advantage this evening, we won't even have the pleasure of listening to her usually sweet notes without huskiness. That won't gain you the prize, Julia."

"I am very glad there are no men to listen to your complaints and regrets," broke in the low voice of Louise Merrington. "Our set of attendants are sufficiently conceited as it is, pray don't let them ever find out how we miss them."

"Pshaw—child, don't you suppose they know it?" at last spoke Laura Stanley, raising her fine grey eyes. "But I have a proposition, Annie, and this old newspaper which you sneer at is my inspiration. I have just been reading the story of some young bachelors who met on a jovial occasion, and vowed a solemn vow that all those who remained single would meet again in ten years' time in that very room, compare notes, and drink a bottle of vinegar as punishment for their neglect of the fairer sex. They sealed up the bottle, and at the close of the two lustres, but one solitary individual—one wretched *old* bachelor—survived of the group. He sat down with the musty bottle and was forced by his conscience to swallow the contents while he read epistles from his fettered friends, detailing their matrimonial experience. Now, suppose we make a compact of a similar nature? Deciding upon the number of years to wait, drawing up the papers, and such, will fully occupy us for an hour or so, and pass the time which you all appear to find so heavy."

"Agreed, agreed," cried every voice.

"But I propose an amendment," said Annie Hamilton. "Let it be 'cherry bounce' or 'maraschino,' not vinegar. I speak, openly I confess it, *mesdemoiselles*, from interested motives, for I dread that fate will cast this drink ultimately upon me, and I have a regard for my teeth and complexion."

"Stop, Annie, before you fly for desk, pen and paper; where is the étui? Hand over."

"What a screw you are, Laura. Here it is, and now to business. Caroline, you who hold the pen of a professor of fine stroke, you who dot your i's and cross your t's. Let Laura dictate and transcribe, we will all follow or copy."

Each busy girl seized a sheet of hot-pressed paper and, with quills or steel pens, as luck or fancy

prompted, was prepared to do her part. Even Miss
Fanny pushed away Bruno, rose to a sitting posture,
and was wide awake in three minutes.

Thus ran the important document which was not
decided upon without much discussion and dispute.

"Oak Forest, December 22nd,
1837.

"We, the undersigned, all spinsters, more or less
young, and all reasonably attractive, do hereby vow
and declare, that on the 22nd day of December,
1847, being ten years from this date, we will meet
in this very spot and drink with much solemnity a
certain bottle of 'maraschino,' in token of our
present friendship and good fellowship. Those who
shall meanwhile have entered into the holy bonds of
matrimony will be excluded, but hereby promise
that, in lieu of themselves, they will send to the
survivors in life and maidenhood, a letter describing
their position as wives or widows. If one of these
below-mentioned subscribers be tempted to forget
her promise, and refuse to come, or refuse to betray
the secrets of her prison-house, or write falsely,
each of the subscribers who faithfully keeps hers,
shall be entitled to claim from the defaulter a
diamond ring. All this being fully settled and agreed

to, we have hereunto set our hands and seals.

Signed,

'CAROLINE MOORE BLOOMFIELD,
LAURA ELIZABETH STANLEY,
ADELAIDE R. CLIFTON,
BLANCHE LOUISE MERRINGTON,
JULIA MERRINGTON,
FANNY STANLEY,
ANNIE HAMILTON."

"Well, I don't consider that a lawyer-like paper, I am sorry to say," said Laura, "but it is my best attempt, though I am a lawyer's daughter. Young ladies, are you satisfied?"

"Perfectly! We are easily pleased, glad young things we are. Now for the maraschino. A glass around, in true club style, to 'our noble selves.' Carry, give us a bottle to seal, and then we shall deposit it with dear Mrs. Bloomfield, with as many directions and cautions, as if it were the regalia of England. Fanny, why so grave?"

"I am thinking of how old I shall be when we open that cordial. Twenty-six! Good heavens, shall I be worth speaking to then? That is what makes me grave, Annie."

"Not the speaking to, little Fan, but the looking at, is what afflicts your young mind. Courage, though, pretty pet; I, with spectacles on nose, for I shall be twenty-eight—and decrepit, of course— shall have the pleasure of reading your letter, signed a happy wife, Fanny Lawrence, and indifferent to age."

"Pray, Miss Hamilton," Fanny was just beginning, when the sound of approaching horses and horsemen, the rapid roll of a swift buggy, the rattling of carriage wheels, many voices, and much laughter announced the approach of a large company, and startled our captivating busy group.

"Girls!" cried Mrs. Bloomfield, through the half-opened door, "the night has cleared a little, and George has brought all the Hunscome party with his own to finish the evening, so make haste, and of course you will have a dance. Mary Hunscome has with her Mrs. William Arnold, and a host of others. Pray smooth your ringlets, and join us as soon as possible. Carry, come to the drawing room first, dear, and see if the ladies would not like to take a chance at your brushes and mirror, after their drive. Where are you carrying that bottle, child?"

"Lock it up, mamma, and I will give you the reason why in ten years," and, with laugh and jest,

and merry musical voices, the pretty band flew to
their rooms. They bared white necks and round
arms, and doffed boots, and donned French slippers.
Some twined garlands of scarlet holly in their
flowing curls. Annie Hamilton looked like a
brilliant Bacchante with her dark tresses bound with
ivy leaves. Fanny Stanley placed a bouquet of
pansies in her glittering hair, and Caroline
Bloomfield shone, as usual, the brightest of all, with
her unadorned braids and snowy dress.

PART II.

Ten years have rolled away. Ten long years to some—passing short to others, and it is now December, 1847.

It is the 4th of the month, however, and not the 22nd, and the scene lies in Charleston, and in a ballroom. Some chance guests—Englishmen—and a Northern *bel esprit*, with her husband, are the reasons given for this unusual occurrence, a large party, a regular February fête at the beginning of December, a time when our city is generally deserted.

The accomplished and witty Northern belle, of course, attracted the most attention, but, next to her, reigned the still lovely, and still enchanting heiress, Miss Bloomfield, of Oak Forest. Twenty-eight summers have passed over her radiant head, and she is in all the bloom of her beauty. She is much changed since I first introduced her at eighteen, it is true, but the change is not to her disadvantage. If the pure complexion has taken a creamy tint, while ten years ago its whiteness had only a rosy shadow, this dusky color shows out with more striking effect the light of her deep blue eyes, the backness of her ever-luxuriant hair, and the vivid red of her beautifully formed mouth. Her figure has now reached perfection. It is amply developed, the shoulders broad yet falling, the bust exquisitely proportioned, and the arms round and polished as they rest upon her harp. She has been singing, this charming Caroline, and, as she strikes the last chords, and the melody of her voice dies away in one long, heart-thrilling note, a burst of thanks ensues from the whole company. But her expressive eyes and lips turn from them to seek the praise which falls quietly and earnestly upon her willing ear, murmured by a person who bends over her with marked attention. He is not strictly handsome, but he is tall and well made, with a decided air of fashion, admirably dressed, short perfumed curls shading a brow of promise, and such eyes!

Perhaps I dwell too much upon eyes, but they go a great way with me. I have a passion for eyes, and no fixed rules as regards my admiration. I have admired green eyes more than I ever shall black or blue ones, and small eyes, where great ones were defying me to find in them a fault. If you tire, my dear reader, of my prosing about these "mirrors of the soul," pray forgive me, but take up the study yourself in your leisure hours, and you will soon begin to watch all your acquaintances visual orbs, as I do mine. But to resume.

These eyes I was about to speak of were very saucy and very handsome, and said fifty different things in as many seconds, when they chose, but now they wished only to repeat the same thing fifty times, so they reiterated, "I adore you," to Carry Bloomfield, till she turned aside, and busying herself with her music, tried to conceal the rising color that spread over her face. "Ah! Caroline Bloomfield at her old tricks," said some kind and observant old lady; "well, she has her match in Edward Allingham—that is one comfort."

At this moment Carolin rose, and, pushing away

her harp, took her companion's arm and allowed
him to lead her towards a recess where a small
table, covered with books, prints and toys, gave
excuse for a lounging flirtation, which two great
arm-chairs helped on. Caroline began replacing her
gloves, and, as she slid the soft leather over her
dainty fingers, Edward Allingham made a petition.
"Pray, dear Carry, let them stay off a moment
longer. I always wish, when I am with you, that
gloves were not; it is only when some one else
appears, and some man looks at or takes your hand,
that I rejoice in these otherwise odious coverings.
Let me see your pretty fingers—what ring is that?"
and bending over so that she was concealed from
the company, he pressed the little hand to his lips,
and tried to slip on her third finger a superb emerald
hoop.

"*Halte là!*" cried Caroline, laughingly
disengaging herself from his grasp; "I am not your
fiancée yet,—and, seriously, Edward, you must
wait, as I have told you, till the 23rd of this month
for my answer."

"What folly!" said Edward, indignantly.

She bowed.

"I beg your pardon, Carry, but you know I love
you, and I hope you love me. What, then, is the

meaning of this?"

"Simply because it depends upon six letters I shall receive on the 22nd, whether I ever marry you or not. Listen to me, Edward—don't start off and look furious, that avails you nothing. On the contrary, listen to me, and I will tell you a secret. Ten years ago, seven young maidens, of whom the eldest was barely twenty, were met together to keep a merry Christmas in an old Southern country house. To beguile the weariness of a leisure hour, the giddy creatures drew up a written document, in which all those who remained single promised to meet at the same spot ten years afterwards and renew their friendship, and talk over their adventures in life, while those of the band who had married, should send, in their places, letters describing their experience of the wedded state. The ten years have passed, and of that happy and thoughtless group, I alone remain in 'single blessedness,' and, singular enough, I have never dreamed of marriage till just when I am on the point of receiving six faithful accounts of six unions, and I have determined to let my decision abide by what I can gather and judge from this trial."

"Do you mean to say, that if any of these six women should happen to have made an unhappy match, you will then conclude that all marriages are miserable, and keep yourself from the chances of such a fate?"

"I mean to say, that if the average of these marriages is unsatisfactory, such will be my decision, for, if half a dozen women, whom I know to have been all well-bred, amicable, agreeable, and lovable, and, what is more, all remarkably pretty, should have failed to find contentment in these 'holy bands,' I cannot hope for a better destiny. But this is scarcely possible, dear Edward. So set your mind at ease, and on Thursday the 23rd, you shall have my answer."

"Foolish woman," said her lover, quite confidently and admiringly, for a moment's reflection induced him to conclude that he ran no great risk. He led her off to dance with as unclouded a brow as if he had already placed the rejected emerald upon the third finger of her right hand.

PART III.

The old dining-room at Oak Forest! Dear,
charming spot! How much brighter it shone, those
ten years ago. Then, such a group of beauties graced
its wide and hospitable table, and now, there was
but our Caroline, alone and somewhat sad. Her head
was pillowed upon her white hand while she lay at
full length upon the sofa, a lamp shedding its
brilliancy just upon her bended brow, and glancing
from it down to six voluminous letters, and a small
dark bottle, scrupulously sealed. Such was the
picture.

There lay the six epistles, and there mused Carry.

Some had come that day—one was a week old—the rest had dropped in during the interval. None had been opened. Caroline drew from the pocket of her cashmere dress a folded paper. It rustled as she smoothed it out, and a delicate perfume of Patchouli escaped from it. It was the contract. A soft smile broke the sadness of Carry's face, and lingered amid the dimples that graced her lips.

"Well, I shall read them, as they come upon the list. Let me see—'Caroline Moore Bloomfield;' here's a striking illustration—the first shall be last. I, who head the train, am the only maiden to keep the agreement. 'Laura Elizabeth Stanley.' Dear Laura, dear noble-minded Laura! What does she say of married happiness? Where is her testimony?" and Carry rose from her lounging attitude, settled the little standing collar that encircled her snowy throat, and while, with one hand, she arranged the heavy folds of her dress around her slight waist, with the other, she searched out the letter which bore Laura's seal. "Now for it."

"Millgrove, *December* 1st, 1847.

"I begin my letter today, my very dear Carry, because, as my quiet home is so far from you, and our mails so irregular, I must allow for all accidents, failures, and stoppages, and give my epistle a full three weeks' start of the eventful 22nd. Is it not strange that you, the handsomest and cleverest of us all, should be the only 'old maid' of the group? And yet it is not strange, for, of course, as the most superior, your claims and expectations were higher —are still—and you have a right to be very fastidious and difficult in your choice.

How well I remember how you looked ten years ago—in fact, how we all looked—when, with girlish frolic, we wrote the famous compact. And the gay dance that ended the evening! How dear Fanny flirted with Willy Lawrence, and how Annie Hamilton protested that Fanny was bent upon showing that she should not drink the maraschino at the appointed time. Poor dear Fanny; she has such a family now! I often ask her if she regrets those carefree days—but I must not tell her answer. That will fill her own letter.

And now to begin my history. You know, dear Carry, that we are far from rich. Mr. Leslie has many debts, and we must live plainly and quietly. My two boys are sturdy fellows, and my little girl is a patter of prettiness and sweetness. She is a great comfort to me. Ned and Harry are at school all the week, and only return home on Saturday. Mr. Leslie is kept much occupied in his fields, and, as I never visit Savannah, which is our nearest city, I see no one but my little Fanny. Mr. Leslie is kind and indulgent to me in all my whims, but he does not fancy books, so that I seldom read, as he prefers seeing me occupied in domestic concerns. My harp has since been 'hung upon the willow,'—that is, I think, three years ago, it was banished to the barn, to make room in our very small parlor for Mr. Leslie's turning-lathe, which interests him very much. As he does not like music, it was no great sacrifice to me to give up my songs. I do a great deal of sewing; my boys are what is called 'hard upon their clothes,' and, therefore, keep me hard at work. I have not touched a pencil or paint brush for years, so you see I am quite a good housewife, and have discarded such frivolous pursuits as accomplishments. In winter, I cannot take any exercise, there being no place to walk except the rice-banks, and Mr. Leslie thinks that women find more wholesome exercise in stirring about the house than in sauntering over rice-banks. During the summer, in the Pineland, I have a saddle-horse, but Mr. Leslie likes his gait so much, that he generally rides him himself, so Fan and I then take rousing walks, and lay in a supply of health and strength for the winter. You see I lead a very humdrum existence, dear Carry, and I dare say you would vote such vegetation 'a horrid bore,' but I am quite satisfied and contented with it. I have shown its sharpest edges and truest colors, so as to write with the candor that we promised each other. I long to see you. I think it is nine years since you were my bridesmaid, and I saw you last. Yes, my twin boys are eight years old, and you have never seen them. Fanny is six. I inclose you a curl of her golden hair. She has eyes as blue as yours, dearest; and such a white skin. Well, I must say goodbye. It is now six months since I wrote to you, and I shame to confess it. Two sweet letters of yours lie by me, unanswered till now. But what can I write to you about? What have I to interest such a dainty creature as 'Miss Bloomfield'—the fascinating 'Miss Bloomfield?' I read an account of your appearance at the Newport fancy ball this last August. One of my Pineland neighbors lent me the Herald. How charming you must have been. Dear Carry, love me always—don't forget your old friend,

"LAURA LESLIE.

P.S. "I drink with you in spirit the first glass of maraschino."

* * *

The letter dropped from Caroline's hand. "Poor, poor Laura! What a fate! Is that a life for anyone to lead! And for Laura, so clever, so accomplished, so refined! No books, no music, no society; nothing but a hard, selfish husband. Can I recognize Robert Leslie in this picture—'Far from rich'—what folly! He is very well off, but he is close and grasping, and he ties Laura down, and they live poor and pinching that he may scrape together a huge fortune —for what? To double it? And yet Robert Leslie was thought a good match. I liked him very much; he seemed very much in love. He gave her fine presents, and it was altogether very suitable—but now…" She read over the letter. It seemed sadder and more touching than before. Tears dimmed her eyes. She sighed heavily, and turned with an effort toward Adelaide Clifton's flowing penmanship. But first the tiny bottle was unsealed and uncorked, and filling a glass, she murmured, "Better times to dear Laura," and touched with her lips the bright cordial.

"Columbia, *December 18th*, 1847.

"Well, dear Carry, the 22nd draws near, and your warning note tells me that I must prepare to fulfill my share of our little compact. I must give you my

history. Lord! my dear child, what can I say? I see
you almost every winter, so that you know a good
deal of my proceedings, and for one who lives such
a dull life as I do, what news have I to transcribe.
You are well acquainted with my liege lord, and
know as well as I do all his whims and oddities. He
is a very good kind of husband, as good as any, I
believe. The only thing very difficult for me to get
over is his dislike for music. I must own, it was very
hard for me to give up my piano. When I thought of
all the time and money wasted upon it, I really
mourned. But John has not the slightest ear, and he
says, besides, that a woman becomes too much
public property when she has people racing after her
to listen to her playing and singing. My two
children show very little musical taste, and their
father rejoices in it. He says that a good
housekeeper had better be in her kitchen than
practicing love ditties. Do you recognize John
Gilmore and his gallantries beside my piano in all
this? Ah, my dear Carry, men change much after
marriage. They say women do—but their husbands
more.

"Another thing I find very hard to stand is, I have
been married barely five years, and yet it is three
since I have gone to a party. John hates balls—he

who was such a dancer and flirter—and it is not the style in this place for married women to go much into company, so we mope at home, and have solemn tea-parties and grave visitings, and are dreadfully dull and proper. Oh dear! It is all very tiresome when one comes to write it down, though life jogs on, somehow, when one does not begin to analyze it. But as we were to write truth, truth I have written, and may you profit. Adieu, dear Carry; if you do marry, try and find out, if you can, what your husband's real tastes are before the knot is tied. I will be in town to spend Christmas with Aunt Elizabeth. Should you return from Oak Forest before the 5th January, you will see

"Your constant friend,
"ADDY GILMORE."

"A health to Addy," said Caroline, and then broke the seal of "Blanche Louis Merrington's" letter.

"Red River, *November* 23rd, 1847.
"Away from the far West comes this token, dear Carry, that I remember our agreement, and that I know you are the only spinster of us all. I will not begin with any usual compliments and questions, for as this will be one of six, you will not care to

wade through many sheets, so I hasten to give you, in as few lines as possible, my experience. You are aware, that through some unfortunate business transactions, we became straitened in our means, and Mr. Radnor determined to move West. We had been married little more than a year (we have only been married now three and a half), and my baby was but a few months old, when we emigrated, and I found everything very dismal and wretched. No neighbors, no society, a church ten miles off, and the nearest city fifty. Our house was small, dirty, unfurnished. I almost screamed when I saw it, but matters improved after a while, and now I am quite comfortable. It is a dreary sort of life, and I long to return to civilization. I miss my summer trips to the North, and whenever mamma writes, telling me that she, and Gertrude, and Lizzie, are off for Newport, I constantly ask Harry if he is worth all I gave up for him. Harry is a nice person, but he is not quite so energetic as I hoped to find him. You know I am not a stirring person myself, so I expect those I am with to stir for me. Harry is so slow. We never would have lost so much had he exerted himself. And then his ideas are so limited. Having lived always with those queer stuffy aunts, he expects everybody to be like them, and therefore looks for old-fashioned

ways and looks in me. He is wedded to his own
notions. To be honest, he is dreadfully stubborn and
horribly afraid of being ruled by his wife, so he is
constantly kicking against imaginary obstacles, held
up to his wrath by possible antagonists. Do you
remember how affable and yielding we used to
think him? 'Harry Radnor will agree to it,' was
always said! Ah, dearest Carry, it is very difficult to
know people before you come to live with them. If
ever you are tempted to choose a husband, bear this
in mind. I never was successful at letter-writing, as
you know, so I plunge this right into the midst of the
business, and having given you a slight picture of
my marriage lines, I will close. We are fast making
money, in spite of Harry's slow ways. So, if we
don't lose it again, you may expect, some time or
other, to embrace once more,

"Your ever affectionate

"LOUISE RADNOR.

P.S. "How is dear Annie Hamilton, and all the
others of our set? I only hear from Julia, poor
thing."

Caroline folded the letter. "What has become of
Lou's sweet temper! How querulous and dissatisfied

is her tone—she who was once the mildest and gentlest of beings. Alas! alas! marriage makes strange changes. A health to Louise. And now for Julia."

"Charleston, *December* 19*th*, 1847.

"I received your note yesterday, dear Carry, with the pretty dress for your name child's Christmas gift, and I join my thanks to hers for your kind remembrance. You reminded me that I owe you a letter, so that, seizing a leisure moment, I hasten to redeem my pledge, given ten years ago. A history of my married life! A true history! You know almost as much as I. Fanny Stanley and I were married within a week of each other, two years after our visit to Oak Forest. Both were love-matches— mine a most ill-advised one. I was headstrong and self-willed. I chose my husband for his handsome person and endearing ways, without one doubt given to the warning voices that bade me recollect his flighty, unstable principles. I loved Edward Calvert, and with the giddiness of barely eighteen, plunged headlong to my ruin. I love him still, dear Carry, and though his death, three years ago, has left me penniless and burdened with the care of two children, I still think he did his best. But he was a

notorious spendthrift who dissipated his own
fortune and mine. Now I am a widow, teaching for
my daily bread, and difficult to be recognized as the
haughty Julia Merrington, who thought this world
and invention got together for her entertainment. I
do not set you against marriage—far from it. They
tell me that Edward Allingham is a suitor of yours.
Is it so? Johnny and Caroline send you showers of
kisses. Where are you reading this? In the dining
room? Ah, those past years! How they rush back
upon one.

"Sincerely and truly,

"your every attached

"J.M. Calvert."

Silently and sadly Caroline laid aside this letter,
and turned to Fanny's. As she broke the seal her
clouded brow and anxious look seemed to say, "not
one happy wife?"

"The Oaks—Santee, *December* 16th, 1847.
"In the midst of all my Christmas preparations,
my dear Caroline, while I was turning over some
old letters to find some waste-paper for the children,
I fell upon a sealed manuscript, and behold, it was

our foolish contract. How it made me laugh!
Charley said, "Mamma, please give me the funny
paper;" so I gave it to him, and no doubt he has
made, if not "ducks and drakes," at least chickens
and boats of it before this. As I do not relish your
coming upon me for a diamond ring, I determined
to sit down and write my letter. If there are any
mistakes, attribute them to Helen, who is
overturning my inkstand every five minutes, and
pulling my hair between whiles. I do not know
exactly what to write about. Am I to give a history
of my married life? It is just like other peoples'. I
have six children, the youngest only four months
old; but this you know quite well. Mr. Lawrence is
very good, and makes a capital husband and planter.
I have a good deal of my own way. We live a great
deal in the country. We quarrel occasionally, but
make it up again. My children give me most
concern. Two of them are far from healthy, and I am
frequently confined to their room for weeks, as
neither Mr. Lawrence nor I can leave them at all to
the care of servants. I am now in all the agony of
deciding whether I will have a governess for my
eldest girls, or send them away from me to town, to
school. This has been the important subject on my
mind for months. I might ask your advice, but how

can a girl decide for the mother of six children? Ah, Carry, perhaps you have chosen the wisest course in remaining single. I am very little my own mistress now, with so many claims upon my attention. I can hardly realize that I am only twenty-six. Why, you are twenty-eight, and as free as the air. Don't misunderstand me, though; I think a woman's surest happiness is found in marriage. The children are calling me, and baby is crying at the height of his voice, so in haste, adieu.

"Yours affectionately,

"Fanny L."

"'A woman's surest happiness—' humph," mused Caroline, "and this is the brightest picture yet. Five letters are over, and there only remains my own dear Annie's. Edward, I fear your chance is small." This was said cheerily, but a bright spot burnt in each cheek, and there was a feverish impatience in her manner as she pushed aide the heap of letters, and opened Mrs. Atherton's. It was the longest of all, filling closely four sides of thin French paper.

"New York, *December* 14, 1847.

"'Hail, hail, all hail,' thou wisest of Carolines!— the only one of seven who has steadfastly kept her much (ought to be) prized liberty—but stop! While I write, a thought comes across me, that perhaps this opening may stand against all future thoughts of matrimony on your part. Far be it from me to thus decide you. Besides, I have just been reading a little story of De Balzac's, which comes so *apropos* I must tell it to you; for, of course, a well-born lady does not read De Balzac herself.

There is a certain young countess who has married her cousin, a colonel under Napoleon; and being very romantically given, when she discovers that after rubbing off his glittering exterior, there nothing remains but a hearty, coarse, good-tempered soldier, she falls into great distress, and loses all her natural happiness. M. le Colonel is ordered to the wars, and leaves Madame under the care of his aunt, a marquise of the old rock who begins to love very dearly her new relative.

One night, when the young countess had retired, more than ever miserable, she bethinks herself of a promise made to an old schoolmate and bosom friend to describe to her her new state—a promise long neglected. Seizing her pen, she begins to write, and the picture was far from flattering to the male sex in general, and to M. le Colonel in particular. In the midst, enter la Marquise, who takes from Julie's passive hand the treasonable epistle, and calmly reads it through. What says the wise dowager? '*A married woman cannot write well for a young person, without missing the proprieties. Because if a dish on the table does not seem right, that is all it takes to disgust a person. Especially my children, when, from Eve to wedding we had something so excellent.*' Julie throws her letter into the fire, and under the tuition of her courtly aunt becomes—well, that is the rest of the story, and regards us no longer.

What I have just written is a case in point. You will, perhaps, wonder why I should really hesitate to write to you (my dearest friend) with that openness and candor we promised each other. But, though you may come down upon me for the diamond solitaire, the price of forfeiture, I am determined. A little bird has whispered in my ear that my fascinating acquaintance, Ned Allingham, is caught at last. Knowing you so well, I begin to fancy that you will not, with your usual caution, let slip this capital opportunity to decide, from others' experience, before you place the yoke upon your own snowy and well-shaped shoulders. So I am silent, and the next steamer will bring you a tiny package. Wear the ring for my sake, and it may, perchance, prove a wedding gift. We are so happy here just now! Can't you come on for a week or two before Lent? I have just bought such a cloak of violet velvet, with a pink bonnet to match—divine! I should so fancy your dear self in them! If you will come, I sha'nt wear them till you get something quite as becoming. Mr. Atherton desires me to add his entreaties to mine. We are a model household (this much I will say), and see each other so little, that we are as pleased to meet as if we were mere acquaintances. Adieu, dear Carry! Though I have already pressed you a great deal to come on this winter, don't hold out in your refusal, but be a good girl, and tell me I may hope to see you before New Year's day. I must close in all haste, for the sun is shining a brilliant request that I should rush to bask in his rays. The horses are ready. My beautiful Zara is pawing up the paving-stones at the door. Mr. Ledyard and John Leigh are patiently waiting till I seal my voluminous letter, so I must don my habit, and ho! for a merry canter to Bloomingdale, while you, mighty and unkind Miss Bloomfield, obstinately refuse to be one of the party. We will put *it* off till you come. Oh! for a telegraph to give your answer.

"Now and ever, your
"Annie."

* * *

Perplexed, tormented, saddened, uncertain what
to do now that she had finished reading the letters,
which she had fondly hoped were to give so much
comfort and decide her fate so easily, Caroline hid
her eyes upon her open palms, and thought, and
thought, till her brain whirled. "I was very, very
foolish," she said, half aloud, "to tell Edward that
these should form my answer. Surely they are not
much in favor of matrimonial felicity, and yet—"
yes, the truth must out: Caroline, like Mr.
Allingham, had had no doubt but that the epistles
would all tend to prove the bliss of wedded life, and
she had demanded the test as a lingering touch of
power, nothing more.

"Pshaw! I will consult with Dora. There is no use
in telling mamma what a simpleton I am, but Dora
is the very person." She rang the bell—"Ask Miss
Dora to come here"—to the servant, summoning her
sister-in-law. Again she pored over the fatal letters.

"Well, Carry dearest," said a sweet, musical
voice, "what do you wish? Here I am. You won't
mind Jim, will you? I was playing with him, and
brought him along. Lie there, my pet, and don't cry,
but be a man, and do as much mischief as you can
quietly." So saying, Mrs. George Bloomfield tossed

her infant son upon a pile of cushions on the floor, flung him her embroidered handkerchief to tear to pieces, and turned to her fair sister-in-law for an explanation. Dora was a New Yorker, small and graceful as a fairy, and pretty as a dream, exquisitely dressed, with a certain air about her whole person and attire that announced the admired belle.

"First, my dear Dora, read that," and Carry handed up the contract.

"Why, I never heard of this wisdom before. How comes this?"

"Oh, I never spoke of it. I had never thought of it till about a month ago; and then—, well, when—in short, Dora, you know Edward Allingham," and Carry told the whole story. How Dora laughed!

"And this is the delicate distress! Poor child! What a prospect! Though you have the united counsel of six wiser heads than mine, and though they all say, as plainly as veiled words can speak, 'Caroline, stay free; Caroline, stay free,' still you wish my tiny voice. Now there remains but one obstacle in my way. What would you like me to say?' And Dora's laughter again rang a merry peal.

"I vow, Dora," exclaimed Carry, "you are incorrigible. Be serious as you can be, and advise me."

"Serious, my sweet sister—oh, Jim, in what a situation is your mamma placed! Don't look at me, young gentleman. If you are tired of my handkerchief, here comes something more," and loosing a gorgeous bracelet from her wrist, it rolled over and over till it reached her baby's feet, who crowed with delight as he clutched the brilliant jewel in his chubby hands. "Profiting by Jim's lapidary tastes, and while he is gravely inspecting my Christmas gift, I will be serious. To remain single, my dearest Carry, is all very well so long as, young and beautiful, you have shoals of admirers and crowds of friends. But in ten or fifteen years from now, with your circle scattered, yourself wearied of outdoor amusements, your contemporaries grown old and retiring, day by day, more into their own shells and houses, you will find yourself alone, shut out from many privileges. No one depends upon you. No life, no happiness is twined closely with your own. There will be George and myself and our children, and 'Aunt Carry' will always be to us a 'personage.' But will Aunt Carry not consider herself as secondary when her feelings and her ambition may wish a first part? You may do a deal of good; your life may be very useful, very cheerful, very full of pleasant duties. But still a mother will always rank you in actual necessity to those around her. You nephews and nieces will love you, love you dearly, but not with that clinging tenderness that belongs to a child's love, that heart-to-heart affection. Are you convinced?

Say then you marry, now comes the rub. Make your choice well. By well, not well in looks or goods alone; never dream of matrimony till you find a man, tender, devoted, whose appearance, manner, rank, means, all please you. Judge if his conversation suits you, if your tastes assimilate, and prefer him to all the world before you say 'I am yours' in the face of heaven and earth. Then prepare to enter courageously upon your new life.

For months be guarded. Do not let a hasty impression of many discomforts with regard to your husband or his family influence your future existence. Question yourself and your own faults. Dwell more on them than on his, as you will soon understand each other. In a word, there is no maxim like the old one, 'bear and forbear.' But, at the same time, should you have been deceived in the man you love,—should it indeed be a nature of tarnishing brass, and not pure gold,—hold fast your woman rights. Yield where you should, and where you shouldn't, be firm.

And hear me clearly: if he is unworthy, part, at once and forever, were it in the honeymoon. Better a life of strict seclusion, a life of mourning and sorrow, than a miserable double existence, dragged on in continual wretchedness, bringing children into the world to follow, possibly, in their parent's footsteps; or, worse still, have some horrible, disgraceful wind-up of an ill-assorted union. Such instances as these are rare, my dearest Carry. A man must be worthless indeed, who, properly managed, changes so much after marriage as some men have done. But their wives have acted foolishly. What was right they should have stuck to, and never have given up what they knew was their just due. As a conclusion, on earth there cannot be greater contentment than in a family where a man and wife truly love, and worthily endeavor to make each other's happiness. I am done."

"Ah! Dora, your marriage is fortunate. George is so good, so kind, you could not be otherwise. He spoils you."

"Spoils me! Nay, Carry, we have learned what I preach, 'bear and forbear;' 'yield and yield.' For instance, George wishes to spend a part of each winter at the South, and I wish to go this summer to

Europe. We will do both—both yield. I wished to learn the polka. George wished me to give up riding Selima, who was very frisky and dangerous. Selima was sold, and I am now a grand dancer—*voila!* Not that this should be viewed in the light of a bargain. But naturally, when we are gratified by a concession, we like to give one in return, and a system which begins in gratitude, ends in conviction. But do you know, I think we northern women make better wives than you southerners. Southern women are apt to be either slaves or tyrants, and themselves aid in making their husbands despots or Jerry Sneaks. They have such a trick of losing their own individuality in the imposing grandeur of the 'he' and 'him' who is the arbiter of their destiny. Prove that I am wrong, and show me what a real Southern wife can do. Come, what answers will you send poor Edward? Your heart speaks for him. Reason speaks for him. Decide,"—and Mrs. George, with a playful gesture, put pen, ink, and paper before her sister, and paused for an answer.

Before that answer came, the dining room door was opened, and Mrs. Bloomfield entered; with her was George.

"A wandering knight claims the hospitality of

these halls," said Mrs. Bloomfield. "I offer it freely, but he awaits your consent, my Carry."

"A consent to more than that, dear, dear Carry," whispered Edward Allingham, as he rushed past his friends to the sofa where sat his mistress.

Caroline drew herself up, hesitated, partly frowned. "Your own hand has penned the answer, my uncertain and doubting sister," said Dora, triumphantly; "while I was delivering my long peroration, your trembling fingers have written on Annie Atherton's letter, 'Dearest Edward,' and then, 'Mrs. Edward Allingham.' I proclaim our blushing Caroline wooed and won."

Mrs. Bloomfield's arms were around her weeping yet happy daughter. Dora's hand rested on her husband's shoulder, who held his handsome Jim close to his heart. And the lover, "too blest for words," looked with glistening eyes at his priceless treasure.

So ends the scene and story.

THE JILTING

CHAPTER I.

A soft breeze was gently sweeping through the closed Venetian blinds. The darkened room was perfumed with the breath of fresh flowers, and a dreamy stillness reigned unbroken. Suddenly a light and hasty step flew along the hall, the drawing room door was quickly opened. A young girl entered.

"No one here, either?" she exclaimed, after a glance around the obscure corners, "no companionship still but my own dull thoughts." She stumbled over an ottoman, and nearly crushed her pretty garden hat, which hung by its broad, pink ribbon from her arm.

"Pshaw, how gloomy it is! Stupid hat, get away," and she tossed aside the unoffending hat, despite the luxury of its deep lace border.

Impatiently the young lady threw open one of the windows, and leaned out.

A thoroughly Southern scene met her gaze. The sun was just setting. No background of mountains hid his last rays—they gleamed only through a veil of pine trees, and lit up here and there a parterre of roses which surrounded the house. The river ran peacefully along between its flat banks, some hundreds of yards off. The rice fields, just beginning to cover themselves with their tender growth, looked fresh and green in the distance, An air of quiet and peace brooded over the whole landscape. Fanny Medwin seemed to care neither for roses nor rice. Her great hazel eyes appeared to scorn all they looked upon. Her full, red lips were curled with anger and disdain, a flush was upon her cheek, and her foot tapped indignantly upon the floor. Very evidently Miss Medwin, though a belle and a beauty, was very near being in a passion.

"I am sure," she said, speaking aloud, "I mentioned plainly enough at dinner that I had a headache, and would not go on the water party. That, I might, perhaps, take a walk at sunset.

Vernon heard me," she paused—"and tomorrow Mr. Lane comes, and then adieu to walks, and drives, and rides for my whole life. Ah, me! To be married in three weeks!" Fanny clasped her hands, and, raising them above her head, they slowly rested on her wealth of golden hair, while a long-drawn sigh heaved her bosom. The sigh was echoed from within the room so distinctly, that Miss Medwin started, exclaiming, "Who is there?"

"It is I, Mrs. Mordaunt, eavesdropping for two good reasons. Come here, darling, and I will tell them to you." The voice was clear, and sweet, and sad. Miss Medwin, partially reassured by discovering who her listener was, walked impetuously towards the sofa, where, hitherto concealed by a screen and some chairs, lay half-reclining the graceful figure of Mrs. Mordaunt. Fanny seated herself upon a footstool close beside the sofa, and taking within her own the jeweled fingers of her friend, asked anxiously, "Are you ill, Mrs. Mordaunt? Why are you not with the others?"

"Perhaps I have a headache, and a walk at sunset may answer for me too," said Mrs. Mordaunt, smiling maliciously. "No," she went on, "that I may confess is not my reason. Seriously, I heard you at dinner, and wished to see the result. Can you forgive me, Fanny, for prying into your affairs? I saw Mr. Vernon leave with the rest of the party, and I was just preparing to go in search of you, when your *brusque* entrance, talking to yourself as usual, induced me to stay quietly here. I wished to show you by experience how dangerous is that habit of thinking aloud, and I also most dishonestly desired that you should say something which would give me an opening for this conversation." Mrs. Mordaunt stopped speaking. Fanny's tiny Paris boot continued to beat time to her own thoughts.

"Fanny, have you never noticed that I take more interest in you than in most young ladies of twenty? Do you not feel that mine is not merely an impertinent curiosity? I am sure you must. Now, I am going to ask you for your whole confidence. Do you love Mr. Lane?"

"No. Yes. Very well—well enough," answered Fanny, removing her chin from the palm of her hand, and looking at Mrs. Mordaunt.

"Do you love Edward Vernon?"

"No," said Fanny, covering her eyes with the disengaged hand.

"I am very glad to hear it," said Mrs. Mordaunt, very slowly, "because he does not love you."

Miss Medwin started, bit her lip, dropped Mrs.

Mordaunt's hand, took it up again, played with a
ruby ring upon the forefinger, and colored. "I know
he does not," she remarked at last.

"You are to be married in three weeks," resumed
Mrs. Mordaunt, "to a man whom you love, 'yes—
no—very well—well enough.' I can promise you
that Edward Vernon will love you then."

Miss Medwin drew up her head, haughtily. "I do
not understand you, Mrs. Mordaunt."

"My dear child," said Mrs. Mordaunt, pressing a
kiss upon the young girl's beautiful brow, and
smoothing her long, fair ringlets, "do you know
how old I am? Candidly?"

"About thirty-six."

"Fanny, I am forty-three, more than twice your
age, and yet, to you, a mere child, I am going to do
what I have never done before to a living mortal. I
am going to tell you my life. Not that it possesses
any charm, so far as stirring incidents, and hair's
breadth scrapes are concerned, but simply as a
warning. Would you like to hear the eventful story
of my life?"

"Very much," said Fanny.

"I shall not begin like Robinson Crusoe, 'I was
born of poor, but respectable parents;' because they
were not poor, though they were respectable. My

mother died about ten years ago. She was an only child, and a beauty. I was an only child, and not a beauty. My mother never forgave me for two things; the first, that I was not handsome, and the second that in spite of my mediocrity of looks, I nevertheless pushed her from her throne when the day came for my presentation to the world as 'grown up.' Though far from enjoying even real prettiness, still I had the effect of beauty. I drew admirers. I was very young, very thoughtless, very imprudent. Men called me witty, women sarcastic. My mother positively disliked me. I got into scrapes without number. I got myself into them, I had to get myself out of them. I laughed and jested with the merriest. I was a mere child, and the world gave me credit for the worst feelings of the worst women. At last my heart, heretofore untouched, became seriously interested in one of my numerous casual adorers. He cared just three straws for me. I amused him. He pleased me. We found ourselves deep in a violent flirtation before we were aware that the town was talking about us. I made no effort to lead him any further. He was poor, as poor as Edward Vernon, Fanny.

"I had not the slightest wish, really, to marry him. I knew he was not in love with me, and I thought I liked him too well to marry him. For, somehow, I had in the depth of my poor, addled brain, a kind of vague, foolish, wicked idea, that a woman should never be in love with her husband. She could not manage him as well, I reasoned. And, moreover, as there must always be more love on one side than on the other, no two people ever loving each other in the same degree, it was far more proper the devotion should all lie on the side of the man. In short, dear Fanny, without being positively 'in love,' I most undoubtedly *preferred* another person when I agreed to marry Mr. Mordaunt, for whom I did not care at all."

"But, why then did you marry him?" asked Miss Medwin, totally forgetting her own position.

A saucy smile passed over Mrs. Mordaunt's face. "Oh, I liked him, I suspect,—very well—well enough." Fanny fidgeted and blushed, but the smile instantly faded from Mrs. Mordaunt's dark eyes, and they were sad with "unshed tears," as she mournfully continued.

"I was very wretched, my child, when I decided upon my marriage. May you never know such unhappiness. I had few friends, none to consult, and many enemies. I was reckless, yet Mr. Mordaunt had long loved me. God forgive me. My relations knew of my indifference to my chosen husband, but they 'trusted to time.' God forgive them. My mother was tired of me, and urged it. God forgive her. My father was absent as usual. Well, I was married." She paused. Miss Medwin felt the tightened clasp of her hand.

"One should never dwell upon any topic too long; so, Fanny, I will pass slightly over the first years of my married life. Suffice it, they were dreadful. How often I wondered at my own blindness, at my own dullness, at my own folly, in fancying that one could endure patiently to live with a person utterly distasteful.

"Mr. Mordaunt loved me. He showed it by his annoying jealousy, his constant attendance by my side; two demonstrations equally to be dispensed with, and neither of which ever inspired a passion in return. His temper was violent beyond belief. When angry, which was generally about three times per day, he overwhelmed me with the fiercest abuse, the grossest insults. What mattered it, that after these paroxysms he loaded me with presents, and implored my forgiveness with solemn promises to be wise and gentle for the future? At first, I trusted in these promises, and really endeavored to love my husband. But woe to her who marries as I did, leaning upon this hope: love after marriage. If the love be not there before the knot is tied, small is the chance that that capricious blind boy should enter the dwelling afterwards.

"It may be that there are women so happily constituted, that they easily resign themselves to circumstances, and with feminine gentleness attach themselves to the stronger arm which the law has made their 'natural protector.' I was unfortunately not one of them. I do not say, but had Mr. Mordaunt been a man whom I could have respected, I might have sauntered along through life, wearily and decently, but I stood in no mental fear of my liege lord, and I confess it with shame, my dear Fanny, I openly and entirely despised him. It is needless to tell my provocations. Though they were great, immense, still had I possessed one spark of holiness I would have borne them more patiently.

"During the first months after my marriage, I seriously contemplated a separation. But those same rumors and scandals which had made me reckless and wretched before this fatal event, deterred me now. I always felt that the world would lay all blame on me—it always does. Did you ever know of a quarrel between man and wife, where society did not take the husband's part? Women too, as has been often remarked, visit with such unremitting severity the conduct of a sister woman under discussion. I was afraid. I was not twenty years old, and I held back, hoping still for 'better times.' I carried my burden to be laid at the feat of the world, that very world whose heartlessness and unkindness had driven me where I was. I plunged into every dissipation offered. I amused myself.

"Meanwhile I had one child." Mrs. Mordaunt's voice faltered, and a shade of unutterable sadness crossed her face. There was a silence of several moments. The light in the room was growing fainter. The evening breeze entering through the one open window, waved slowly to and fro the bright chintz curtains. A ray of departing sunshine gleamed upon the quiet pair. Mrs. Mordaunt's face was a study. There was a dreamy depth in her large eyes, and her brow was so calm with all its sadness.

"I had one child," she resumed, "a dear little girl, but she did not fill my heart. You may not think me attractive, Fanny, and wonder to hear it—but still such is the fact: I had shoals of admirers. My manners were frank and easy. I was sufficiently clever to pass for a 'great wit,' in a circle not renowned for its brilliancy. '*In the kingdom of the blind, the one-eyed is king*,' as they say. I was superficial enough not to frighten the ignorant. I dressed well, danced well, and sang passably; in short, I led the fashion.

"So passed four years. Gradually my shoulders grew accustomed to the tiresome matrimonial yoke, which a sad fate, a joyless home, and my own inexperience had placed there. I learnt to manage my husband better that I had done in those first wretched days, when, conscious of his injustices, I indignantly received his insults and submitted to his anger. Now, I asserted my rights, and forced him to treat me with more respect. This had a good effect with him. He learnt to fear me too, and I began to enjoy my life more than I had ever done.

"But what a frantic career of vanity I now ran. My pretty Helena was not positively neglected. She was constantly at my side, a plaything, a pet, a charming accessory to the picture. Her shining black braided hair, her violet eyes, and exquisite complexion, set off by the thousands luxuries of her dress, played a distinguished part in my daily exhibitions. Lounging in my carriage, displaying to admiring eyes a wardrobe of unexceptionable taste, nothing filled up the scene better than Helena, on the front seat, in her velvet robes and capotes of drawn satin, dividing her attention between the fit of her tiny gloves and the long ears of my Blenheim, which lay beside her. Then on a spring afternoon, invariably mounted upon a diminutive pony, she cantered at my elbow, while I rejoiced the sight of the bystanders with my excellent horsewomanship. But, except as a toy to be admired, a gaudy puppet to be fondled and adorned, the poor little thing had no very firm place in what I was pleased to call my heart.

"Had I been less worldly, had I not been scared to the bone by the ill usage I had passed through, Helena could have been now to me, all and everything. So beautiful, so clever, so engaging— what dearer or more interesting occupation than to train that young life to blossom into sweetness and into excellence! She was to have masters in several languages, to be taught music and dancing, so soon as her age permitted, and thus time went on. I grew more and more frivolous, less and less inclined to take a sober view of my duties.

"Enemies, jealous of my seeming happiness, little knowing the home agonies I endured, sprung up around me. The same detractors who had wantonly injured my reputation before my marriage were prepared with tales quite as harsh now. I equally despised them and their stories. Secure in my true innocence, I defied their sneers and reports, and took no pains to either smooth over my imprudences, or to deprecate their insinuations. Most unfortunately my contempt for gossiping, my knowledge of its almost inevitable lies, would not permit me to dread its power of evil. We do not often fear what we despise.

"An occurrence that took place about this time, taught me how absurd it was ever to pay the least attention to the world's opinion. Two young girls became engaged the same winter. One of them, a Miss Black, was forced through the decided ill-health of her lover to dissolve her engagement. A marriage contracted under such circumstances would have been like uniting the dead body to the living one. Like all consumptives, he had no idea of his own state, and urged their union; so much so, that her family found no means to block him off, than to break the engagement 'till his better health.' She retired from society, and paid no visits. Two months after, he died. Miss Black put on half mourning, such as one would wear for a cousin. The engagement of Miss Dallas, the other young lady, was private, and only declared when her fiancé was on his death-bed. Miss Dallas donned the deepest weeds. There were both fiercely, equally, and virulently abused. Miss Black was apostrophized as heartless, unkind, indecent. Miss Dallas, as absurd, ridiculous, indelicate. The one was compared to the Chinese widow fanning her husband's grave to dry it up the day after his internment—the other was dubbed 'the virgin widow,' and laughed at accordingly.

"'Talk to me again,' I said to an old bachelor friend, after listening to a conversation which had for its subject both of these ladies—'talk to me again of regarding the world's opinion and regulating your conduct to its standard! What standard? It vilifies Miss Black for mourning too little, and Miss Dallas for mourning too much, in the same breath. It rails against me now because I am happy, and love balls and dancing. Were I to quiet its 'busy scenes,' and domestically retire, it would accuse me of concocting *des horreurs* beneath the shady privacy of my home.'

"'This may well be, dear,' replied my old friend, 'but you are wrong, nevertheless. Doubt the justice of the world as much as you choose. Condemn it as inconsistent; sneer in your own heart at its aptitude to be duped, in spite of its supposed wisdom, but learn to manage the opinions. Like you, my dear, I hate the world, I despise it, but—I fear it.'

"Would that I had lent an attentive ear to the sage advice of my good Mr. Stanley! It was about a week after this very speech, that a stranger destined to play a conspicuous role in my history visited our city. Don't you find it warm in this room, Fanny," said Mrs. Mordaunt, suddenly interrupting herself, and rising quickly from the sofa, "let us go into the air. This place chokes me, somehow."

Miss Medwin silently acceded. They passed through the piazza into the flower-garden, and Mrs. Mordaunt led the way towards a green turfy path which ran zig-zag down to an ornamental spring.

"How fresh it is here!" she exclaimed, "and so calm, so sweet! Look at that bird, Fanny and as I live, a real summer butterfly! Shall we catch it?" There was an unusual flush on Mrs. Mordaunt's cheek. Miss Medwin could not but notice her heightened beauty, but she wished to hear the rest of the story.

"Dear Mrs. Mordaunt," she said, "are you not going on?"

"Not tired, Fanny, of my twaddle?" Well, where was I? Oh, yes! A stranger came to pass the season in the city. Mr. Frederick Arlington was his name, and he was, certainly, the handsomest man that ever a woman dreamed of. He was well-born, well-bred, accomplished, agreeable, well-read, without pedantry, and *insouciant* without frivolity. You may wonder what possible blemish there could be in this perfect creature. He was thoroughly selfish, heartless, and deceptive; but it needed a long acquaintance to bring to light even such very decided faults as these, so dazzling the exterior. He was a man capable of letting his best friend die at his door (provided he was unperceived), and the next moment, his thrilling, manly tones would give additional weight to some noble sentiment.

"Mr. Arlington was received among us, almost with open arms. He was quite the rage. Seeing him the object of general attention, my vanity was aroused to secure him to myself. I wished to bring this courted youth irretrievably into my net. I wished to be sure, that whatever invitation beset him, he would throw over ball, beauty, or billiards, to obey the slightest signal from me. I wished my rivals to see that my charms were irresistible. I wished Mr. Arlington to go away, thinking me an adorable woman. But, for my own part, of course, I was to remain as ever, cold, impassive, unimpressionable, and as calculating as a dowager of fifty, with six unmarried daughters. A few glances, a few soft, meaningless words, soon brought Mr. Arlington to my side, and in a little while my coquetries had, as I thought, secured my prize. He was my devoted slave.

"But scarcely had I triumphantly exhibited him during one evening in my train, that I felt him slipping through my fingers. Fred Arlington was too old a bird to let himself be caught by such chaff as my nothing-promising looks and words. He let me feel the charm of his manner and conversation, and then coolly bowed himself off. I was piqued. 'Pray, where is Mr. Arlington?' I was asked by impertinent Mrs. Charlton, at a ball. 'Is it true that he says he does not like flirts, especially married flirts?'

"'Was Mr. Arlington consigned to me when he came here?' I replied, nonchalantly, 'and are there such things as married flirts?'

"'Oh, you ought to know,' answered my interlocutor, 'but I have heard that Mr. Arlington says he is disappointed in you, after hearing so much of you. I think it very rude of him. You must feel very much mortified.'

"'How fortunate, then, that you will never suffer from the pangs I am enduring, because it is not likely that you will ever be mentioned by any stranger.'

"Mr. Arlington entered just as I made this rude

speech. I presume the feeling that brought it forth, though not commendable in itself, had the effect of producing a becoming luster in my eyes. He looked at me with rather an admiring air, and not long after came to ask for a dance.

"I played his own game back to him. No more tender glances. No more little encouraging words, which he had discovered to mean only—'So far shalt thou go and no further.' I was so playfully indifferent, so deliciously agreeable, and so plainly indicative of 'fancy free.' As for making a reproach, or hinting at his late absence, no such bourgeoisie idea came into my head. I was simply a very clever, rather pretty, decidedly fascinating and vastly entertaining little woman, doing 'the proper' to a distinguished stranger, but thinking rather more of a handsome, conceited boy, planted at my right, than of the tall Englishman on my left.

"Mr. Arlington was nettled in his turn. Not to pursue so commonplace and ordinary a style of thing, it all ended as you may suppose—in his renewed devotion, but not in my renewed advances to meet it. I played the part of an agreeable but strictly virtuous wife to perfection. I even deceived so experienced a hand as Frederick Arlington. He began to think he was mistaken in me. I was not the daring coquette, hardened by a long series of epidermal flirtations, that he had thought me. Like all 'fast' men of his class, Mr. Arlington had no idea of expending the ammunition of his attentions upon a married woman for nothing. He had no idea of being treated like a pleasing novelty, talked to, smiled at, cajoled, and then dismissed when he became serious. I trust all this is new to you, Fanny. I trust the corruption of the world is as yet a sealed book to your young mind, and assuredly it is only as a warning, as a lesson, that I venture to lay open to you such wickedness.

"Well, the town began to whisper as usual, first low, then loud, about this new flirtation of Mrs. Mordaunt's. As usual, also, I flattered myself, and soothed my convenient conscience by knowing that, except an occasional permitted kiss upon my hand, Mr. Arlington was allowed no favor inconsistent with propriety. The gossips might count how many times per day he entered our house, how many rides per week he took with me, and how many hours he lounged away in my carriage while I was visiting or shopping. All these items had only been to me matters of supreme indifference."

Mrs. Mordaunt stopped to pluck a blade of grass from a tuft at her feet, she wound it round and round her fair fingers. The fixed earnestness of Miss Medwin's look seemed to embarrass her.

They sauntered quietly along. The spring of fresh bubbling water was before them; and the lingering twilight enveloped in a dreamy haze the long-leaved aquatic flowers that bordered the ledge of this natural fountain. The elder lady sat down upon a rustic bench. Fanny Medwin placed herself in her favorite position at the feet of her friend, her elbow resting upon Mrs. Mordaunt's lap.

"I need not, I hope, protest to you, my dearest child, that nothing but my love of admiration first drew me into undertaking so dangerous a pastime as flirting with Mr. Arlington; but, alas! I must admit that gradually I began to take a new and singular pleasure in his society. Why deny it now? Why offer a garbled confession? Better tell the truth at once. I fell—yes, it was a fall—I fell desperately in love. I, who had passed heft-whole through a dozen declarations, acknowledged reluctantly, almost fiercely, that my future happiness—my future life, was bound up in Frederick Arlington. To myself, not to him. To him I still tried to appear a warm friend, nothing more. 'How has this come about?' I mentally asked. 'Is he so far superior, so far above all the men I have ever known?' As if one ever heard or read of love that came because of this or that. 'You love because love,' is too true to argue upon.

"Vainly I struggled against this growing feeling, and I presume the first real indication Mr. Arlington had of his success were my efforts to avoid him.

"About this time a fancy ball, which had long been in preparation, came off. It was to be a very grand affair. My costume had been decided upon weeks before. When I stood in front of my cheval glass on the eventful evening, I felt the delicious consciousness that I was looking my very best. And with that delicious consciousness came back upon me the dreadful reality, that on the morrow, Mr. Arlington was to leave the city. His last impressions of me would be favorable to my appearance, but they would be his last."

"What did you wear?" asked Miss Medwin, with feminine curiosity on so important a subject.

"I was dressed as a Marquise of Louis XV.'s time, and with my powdered hair, my pencilled eyebrows, my rouge, and my magnificent brocades; no wonder that my waiting-maid was lost in admiration. On entering the ball-room, Mr. Arlington came to me. His dress corresponded to my own, and even accustomed as every one was to his remarkable beauty, I assure you a murmur of admiration followed him. His grace, his courtly air, the indescribably elegance of his manner and address were perfectly irresistible. How my guilty heart beat with pleasure as he bent his stately head before me! 'How bewilderingly pretty you are this evening,' he whispered; 'you dance with me, of course, the first? And how many more? Shall you venture to waltz in that preposterous little train? Positively, it makes you so tall I stand in awe of you.' And I listened and smiled, and felt so subdued, and so supremely happy. What a brilliant ball it was!

"After supper, Mr. Arlington persuaded me to take a stroll through all the rooms. There was one small chamber fitted up as a boudoir; silk and satin, and bull work tables, and marquetry writing desks, with large china vases and pastille burners diffusing incense.

"What is the use of trying to put off the evil moment, by describing all this luxury? In that sweet retreat, entirely abandoned and left alone to us, we sat down, and Mr. Arlington spoke of his approaching departure.

"He took my hand, hoped we would be always good friends, and looked into my eyes. What followed next, I cannot remember. Suffice it, he declared his love, and I acknowledged mine. I knew he was to leave the next day. What mattered it, that he should carry away the certainty from my own lips of my foolish, wicked preference.

"But scarcely had my faltering tongue confessed my crime, when Mr. Arlington's arms were around me, and, recklessly yielding to my temporary madness, I suffered his passionate embrace. An exclamation aroused us both. I sprang to my feet just in time to see the vanishing head of one of the most intolerable gossips of the city, and my bitterest enemy.

"'See how absurd it is now, how useless, to fight against your fate? Dearest Emily, fly with me! Certainly I would rather have owed your concession to your love alone; but that woman hates you so intensely that it would be utter folly to trust her honor, or to brave her scandal.' It is needless to pursue his argument and my weakness. I consented. I consented to go with this stranger—to leave my child, my friends, my parents, my husband. But I falsely argued, except to my child, I owed no duty. What friend stepped forward to save me from a hated marriage? Which parent hesitated to urge the union? What a husband had I? A man who ground me to the earth, while I was timid and fearful, and who was subservient now, because I crushed him.

"All arrangements were hurriedly agreed upon, and then we parted.

"Night is coming upon us, dear Fanny, and I must hasten to the end. The ball was on Wednesday. On Thursday morning, Helena, as if by instinct, seemed unwilling to quit my side. The hour had struck—I must be off. I rang for Helena's maid, and ordered her to take the child for a walk. The little girl returned with such clinging fondness my shower of kisses, that my heart wavered. I hope—I have always hoped—I must hope, that it was in that instant I changed my mind. I resolved to bear all ills for her sake—for the sake of my little Helena. Surely I could not have left that sweet child—I never could have done it. Her arms so silently implored me to cast my own protecting ones around her so long as I should live." The tears streamed down Mrs. Mordaunt's face. "Can a mother forsake her only child, and that a girl? Oh, Fanny! say you think it was then I changed my mind! Helena's cheek was pressed to mine. 'Goodbye, then, dear, pretty mamma.' A confused noise was in the hall— men's feet tramped up the stairs—voices in loud whispers spoke my name—I threw open my bedroom door, and stood face to face with the dead body of my husband!"

"Great heaven!" exclaimed Miss Medwin.

"Was it not horrible? I believe I fainted. The shock was so sudden, my spirits so unequal, my position so strange. Mr. Mordaunt had died in a fearful manner. It appeared that he had always suffered from an affection of the heart, and now he had fallen to the gourd, dead, while speaking to an acquaintance in the street.

"Friends flocked around me. Offers of service were abundant. I was not needed, so I lay for days upon my bed in a darkened room, holding Lena's little fingers tightly in my own, and apparently dozing with half-shut eyes. But my mind was wide awake. God had mercifully snatched me from the commission of this great crime. I was wicked enough, but not irretrievably lost. The interest of my state, a widow with a large fortune, and only one child, served to deaden the voice of scandal. Miss Weston, the prying old maid, found but few listeners to her wonderful boudoir tale, and of those few, half of them doubted it. I heard my cousins whispering about it, as they sat croning over the fire in my bedroom. 'What an idea! and she, poor child, mourning so sincerely for Harvey Mordaunt. But then old women must always find something new.'

In my heart I was full of thankfulness. Not that for my own sake I was spared the world's prejudices, but for my Helena's. She was to be my future care —my future hope—my future life—darling Helena! I thought of Frederick Arlington with a shudder. To associate his name with love would have seemed like choosing an open vault for a nuptial chamber. The same muttering voices in conversation had already taught me that he had left at his appointed time on the fatal Thursday, though apprised of the sudden event. How deeply, yet mournfully thankful I had a right to be!

"The funeral over, the nine days' wonder died away, and my widow's cap of a most scrupulous severity, I shut myself up to arrange my plans. In my own mind, there were soon settled. I appointed strict and honorable trustees for my property, not choosing to undertake the management of so large an estate myself, and Helena's education began in earnest. I received only the visits of intimate friends. I went nowhere. My conduct was modeled after the most prudish standard.

"Three years of this life won me the reputation of a grave and dignified woman. Scandal would have searched in vain for any crevice to pick at, in the even marble of my life and conversation. At last, when Helena was ten years old, I announced my intention of taking her to Paris. To shorten my long story, we went, and there I spent the next six years." Mrs. Mordaunt nervously hurried her voice. Her lips trembled.

"One night, at the Italian opera, I met Frederick Arlington. He joined me and we renewed our acquaintance, reluctantly on my side. But at length my innate coquetry had the triumph of bringing him to my feet, after a neglect of so many years. I rejected him, of course. My heart was dead to such love. Maternal idolatry had superseded every other passion. I adored my Helena, and nothing but that which concerned her could interest me. Springing up into early womanhood, graceful as a ballet dancer, but simple and modest as a wild flower. Earnest and truthful as we fancy angels, but arch and merry as a little fairy, she was more attractive than any creature I ever saw. Her beauty, perfect as it was, was indeed her least charm. So sweetly happy, so bright, so affectionate, so accomplished, I never could decide in which position she pleased me most—whether sitting at my feet, her small white hands crossed over my knee, he violet eyes fixed on mine, as yours are now, dear Fanny; or standing by her harp, her stately young head partly turned from me, and her glorious voice filling the room with its overpowering melody.

"But I could go on for ever, describing the alternation of her character and pursuits. I am trying to postpone the fatal moment, and I only wring my own heart with the recollections of her piety, her virtue, her sweetness, her loveliness. She was just seventeen; she was all that the most exacting mother could desire; she was the admiration of the high-born society in which I moved; she was my all— and she died. Yes, my Helena—my pride—my idol. She died after a few days' illness—died with my despairing arms around her—died as she had lived; innocently, uncomplainingly, entirely beloved."

Fanny Medwin's tears were flowing with her friend's. "You pity me, Fanny. Yes, to this day, I need your pity. Was I not punished? My sin had found me out. From the brain fever under which I lingered for weeks after my Lena's death, I arose a broken-spirited, but, I trust, a better woman. My life since my widowhood had only been a well-acted play—now it was a reality. Hitherto I had inwardly sneered at many of the pruderies and religious observances, which care for Helena had made me practice. Now, my dead child seemed to whisper to me from above, 'Live and feel, dear mother, so that we may be again united.' Years have rolled with their ceaseless surge over my sorrow-bowed head. I have not given up society; I live in what hypocrites, with well-feigned disdain, call 'the world.' I am honored. I am respected. I try to do good. I try to be good. I love all young girls for my Helena's dear sake.

"I was first drawn to you by a likeness, real or fancied, in the turn of your head, and in your walk, to my lost darling. Love me, Fanny—love me with your whole heart, if you can. I will never desert you. I am rich. I have power. You have no father and your mother has other children. Break off this engagement in which you heart has no share. Never marry as I did. Listen to me: I sail for Europe next week. Come with me—be my companion—my solace, till you meet a man worthy of you. I do not say, be my daughter, for that sacred name belongs alone to one; but in all save the name of daughter will I cherish and protect you. Are you willing, Fanny?"

Excited, carried away by her feelings, Fanny's first impulse was to accept this generous offer. For she was tenderly attached to her friend, and, moreover, to live with Mrs. Mordaunt was to open to the ambitious girl a brilliant field of conquest and distinction. But her mother must be consulted, and through her still swimming tears she explained this.

"Set your mind at ease on that score, my dear love," said Mrs. Mordaunt. "Mrs. Medwin and I have long since discussed the whole business. I have her consent. You are not to look upon this as a formal attempt to separate you from your family. We will often all be together, and, God forbid, that I should try to wean you from them. Kiss me, dear Fanny, and now we must think of home and our hostess, and smiles and laughter. Tomorrow morning, before Mr. Lane arrives. We will be on our way to town. Leave a letter for him, and your mother will see him"

"But, dear Mrs. Mordaunt, though I do not love Mr. Lane, I fear he will think me very ungrateful. He has been so devoted, so considerate, so submissive to all my whims, that though my spirit bounds with joy at the prospect of my release, still he will have reason in accusing me of unkindness and cruelty."

"What mistaken kindness in you it would be to marry him, my poor Fanny. Is it not far better that he should now suffer a momentary pang, than that you should both pass through such a life as is led by ill-assorted couples? Do you not think that later,

even he might regret your want of resolution, when
he discovers that you never loved him. When he
learns that you sacrificed yourself, and tied him to
an unappreciative wife, when in this wide and
populous world, he might have found some doting
woman who would love him for himself alone.
Believe me, dear Fanny, in real life, such marriages
never answer. Even supposing that love should
come, it can never be the love that ought to exist
between a husband and wife. Every man will think,
sooner or later, that if he had not been deceived, or
deceived himself into fancying a reciprocal passion
in the lady of his choice, he would have discovered
this latent spark in some other woman."

With a sight of relief at finding her objections so
easily swept away, Fanny place her hand within the
grasp of Mrs. Mordaunt's. She was almost
convinced that, in jilting Mr. Lane, she was doing
him the kindest service. Can critics determine if she
were not?

Fanny and her friend walked home by the light of
the old stars. They walked sadly, yet it was a
mellow sadness. The solitary heart of the widow
had found an object on which to rest. Miss Medwin
seemed to have grown even younger, since her feet
trod the path a short half hour before. Their sadness

was natural. Mrs. Mordaunt had recalled bitter scenes. Miss Medwin had wept for and with her friend.

The drawing room of Clermont was bright with the blaze of candles, and with the shining eyes of many beauties, when our two friends entered it, just before tea. Mrs. Mordaunt took her seat at the open piano and ran her fingers rapidly over the keys.

"Hush, good people" she said, "pray stop talking about your water party. Sailing on the river is a very good thing, but I claim your surprise, at least, and your good wishes for a longer voyage. Miss Medwin and I leave you tomorrow morning at daybreak, and these fair shores on the 20th. Come, 'Here's a health to the outward-bound.'"

Even the charm of Mrs. Mordaunt's singing could not restrain whispers. There was a general exclamation. And there we leave them.

On the appointed day, Mrs. Mordaunt and her charge sailed from New York.

Six months have elapsed. Mr. Lane was inconsolable. He is beginning to recover.

Edward Vernon speaks of going to Paris. Unless for his own pleasure, he may as well not.

One moonlight night at sea, as they sat chatting beneath its bright beams— "Tell me, Aunt Emily," said Fanny, "why did you say on that memorable afternoon, that, should I ever marry, Edward Vernon would love me then?"

"Because, my own little Fanny, Edward Vernon is such a man as I once described to you. What prevented him from long ago usurping Mr. Lane's place?"

AN EPISODE IN THE LIFE OF A WOMAN OF FASHION

AN EPISODE IN THE LIFE OF A WOMAN OF FASHION

"At home this evening, madam?"

The lady slightly started, turned her head, yawned, and looked indifferently at the questioner.

He was a servant in livery, as black as Warren's blacking, and with an air of great pomposity and distinction, as became his dignity of butler in a well-ordered establishment.

Finding his mistress gave no answer, Hector repeated his question.

"Yes. Why do you ask, Hector?"

"Mrs. Somerton has sent to say that if you are at home she will come round and see you, madam."

The lady shrugged her shoulders, and made a light grimace.

"Certainly. I shall be happy to see Mrs. Somerton. And, Hector, let my coffee be *very* strong presently."

Hector closed the drawing-room door softly behind him, and the lady of the mansion gave another long yawn.

She was very pretty, this lazy little woman. Small, graceful, and beautifully made; so fair, so white, and yet so brilliant, with red lips and wicked eyes, and black lashes and eyebrows, and golden-yellow hair.

Her features were not regular, but then they were so expressive, and there was such sauciness in her glance, and in the dimples that incessantly played around her mouth. You could not criticize, you could only admire. She was about twenty-five, and looked twenty. The drawing room was handsomely and tastefully furnished. It was well lighted, and had that cheerful, inhabited look which books, and work, and flowers give. The mistress of all these possessions sat immediately below the chandelier, carelessly playing with the charms that hung from her *chatelaine*, and evidently not thinking of them. She was charmingly dressed, and seemed to have no objection to disclosing occasional glimpses of her lovely shoulders, which were partially covered by a scalloped dress of pale blue silk. Her bare arms glittered with bracelets, and diamonds were profuse upon her hands.

Slowly and dreamily did the miniature dangling cups, keys, trumpets, and fans drop, one by one, through her small white fingers.

At last she rose, sauntered to a mirror, and gazed earnestly at the reflection of her own dear little person.

"Upon my word," she exclaimed aloud, "I do believe I am growing old. I 'must keep earlier hours, and live more soberly,' as Rosa writes. What a jest! As if anything but a cabbage or a dormouse ever had less life than I rejoice in now. Oh, for a sensation! Something to rouse me from this dull vacuum. How stupid all the men were last night! Not one of them deserved the toilette I made."

She took up a bouquet of rare flowers, picked off a dead leaf or so, hummed a polka, and then the street door-bell rang with emphasis.

"There is Mary Somerton! Now for three mortal hours of twaddle." After a bustle in the passageway: "My dear Mary," said the little hypocrite.

"Annie, my love, allow me to present Mr. Lascelles. Mr. Lascelles, my friend, Mrs. Montrose Grey." And the triumphant Mrs. Somerton, a tall, showy, silly woman, did the honors, and enjoyed the surprise of her friend.

Mrs. Grey, as she welcomed her guests, acknowledged to herself that the new-comer was the handsomest man she had seen for a very long time, and wondered where on earth Mrs. Somerton had picked him up.

"So, Annie, you are not going to the Lesters' ball tonight! How is it that you are in a stay-at-home mood?" said Mrs. Somerton.

"The Lesters' parties are invariably so dull, one loses nothing, and gains an affliction of ennui by frequenting them, not to mention the danger one runs of someday falling into the large and always open mouths of those fine-teethed girls," replied Mrs. Grey.

"Severe as usual, my dear; I am so afraid of you! Don't alarm Mr. Lascelles beforehand. He has promised to be there at ten o'clock, and rather enjoyed the prospect just now."

"That was when I hoped Mrs. Grey would kindly take charge of me," said the stranger, speaking for the first time, and in a voice of the most peculiar intonation. There was almost a tremor in its musical depth.

Annie raised her eyes inquiringly to his face. He was grave, quiet, gentlemanly, and, with all his beauty, had not the faintest tinge of conceit in his bearing. "Really," she began—

"Cannot you change you mind, and chaperone Mr. Lascelles?" interposed Mrs. Somerton; "you know my mourning"— glancing down at a rich black silk, garnished with beading—"prevents *my* going."

Annie Grey laughed merrily. "Positively, you wish me to assume the responsibility of an unknown gentleman, my dear Mary? Mr. Lascelles looks highly respectable, I am willing to admit; but I will not promise to shine at the Lesters', with this twin star by my side" bowing with mock admiration, "until I find out who he is. Mr. Lascelles, who are you?"

Mrs. Somerton looked aghast. She never could quite understand her saucy friend's speeches; but Mr. Lascelles answered, with great gravity, "I am the eldest son of an English gentleman, who is well connected, and as highly respectable as I look. My name is Charles. I am traveling for amusement. I have letters to many of *the* most remarkable men of this country. The British consul here is answerable for me. My credit at my banker's is unlimited. I am twenty-eight years old, and a great admirer of Mrs. Montrose Grey."

"Most satisfactorily answered," said Annie; "but when have you learnt to admire me?"

"That I shall tell you when you take me to Mrs. Lester's."

"It's a bargain, then," said Mrs. Grey, as she rang for the coffee, which was no longer needed *very* strong, for Mrs. Somerton's dreaded prosing had not the usual effect. To the sweet water of her style Mr. Lascelles was the spirit, and Mrs. Grey the acid, which made up a charming mixture of conversation punch; and so they chatted on, till it was time to dress.

"I will call at your hotel for you," said Annie to Mr. Lascelles, as he and Mrs. Somerton rose to take leave.

"A thousand thanks."

Mr. Lascelles offered his arm to his companion as they crossed the street. "Will it be thought singular," asked the gentleman, with his English prudish manners, "for Mrs. Grey to stop for me alone?"

"She will not be alone, my dear, sir; Mr. Grey

always goes out with Annie."

"Mr. Grey?" exclaimed Charles Lascelles, stopping abruptly, "who is he?"

"Her husband, of course. Did you take Annie for a widow?"

Mr. Lascelles scanned the lady's face by the gaslight. "Are you jesting?"

"Not in the very least," replied Mrs. Somerton, laughing heartily. "Annie has been married for five or six years, and Mr. Grey is devoted to her. I shall fancy that you are in love with her, Mr. Lascelles; and *apropos*, what was that about admiring her, which you were to explain this evening?"

"A mere piece of nonsense," said the Englishman, in a tone of gravity which he vainly tried to render indifferent. "Mrs. Grey has very disengaged and unencumbered manners, and I naturally thought that she was a widow. She is very pretty," he added. "Here we are, at your house. Many thanks for your kindness."

"Will you walk in?"

"No. I have barely time to reach my hotel and dress. The first turning to the right, is it not? *A bien tot.* Good night." And, with a hurried bow, Mr. Lascelles departed.

The last touch was given by the skillful fingers of

her French waiting-maid, and Annie looked complacently at the exquisite termination of their united labors.

The dress was of tulle, with a myriad of skirts, falling one over the other, and yet so admirably managed, that, like the jupes of a ballet-dancer, no bunchiness disfigured the slight yet plump contour, and the effect conveyed was a kind of cool haziness most refreshing to the eyes. At regular distances, upon three of these flounces were embroidered silky wreaths of water-lillies, done in their natural colors of white and green; and just where began the graceful line of the corsage in the centre of the bust, a shower of large pearls was clustered, which, gradually decreasing down to the slender waist, ended at the point. The rich hair was wound smoothly at the back of the head; and the bandeaux, parted with seeming carelessness in front, waved in bewitching undulations, and were confined by a garland of artificial water-lillies to match those of the skirt. A necklace and bracelets of pearl completed the costume, which would have suited some Naiad, and which the adorable freshness of Annie Grey set off and adorned.

A tap at the door announced the carriage ready, and "monsieur waiting *au salon* for madame." Mrs.

Grey swept softly into her husband's presence, and resting her little white hand upon his arm, while Louise put on her over-shoes, said,

"Mrs. Somerton begs us to take an Englishman to the Lesters'. We will pick him up in passing. It is a Mr. Charles Lascelles. Thank you, Louise, my fan and bouquet."

Mr. Montrose Grey was a subdued, insignificant-looking man, not ugly, nor in any manner conspicuous.

"You are very pretty tonight," he remarked to his wife, and bent his lips towards her forehead; but a slight movement on her side caused the kiss to slide off to her glittering hair, which it slightly discomposed.

She smoothed it at the mirror, and humming a gallop, proceeded to the carriage.

"Quite ready, Mr. Lascelles? Or have I made you wait?" she asked, as that gentleman, wrapped in his paletot, emerged from the hotel door. "Allow me to present Mr. Grey."

"Happy to meet you, sir," said the husband of the supposed widow, and then relapsed into total silence. Mr. Grey was evidently not the talking partner of his firm.

Annie was. She rattled on with great gayety,

describing the peculiarities of the people they were to see, naming the celebrities of the place, recommending the most agreeable women, and praising the best men.

She felt Mr. Lascelles' arm slightly tremble as he assisted her from the carriage, and again as she took it on entering the ballroom. "Are you cold?" she innocently asked, looking up into his eyes.

"I? no." And an actual blush flushed his cheek while going through his presentation to Mrs. Lester, who, being the mother of many sons and daughters, thought it but respectable to wear, even on so festive an occasion, only the veritable black silk in which she had done her household's shopping for many years, and a plain muslin cap, guiltless of ribbon or flower.

"Do you dance? Shall I provide you with a partner?" demanded Mrs. Grey.

"Won't you dance with me yourself?"

"Yes, the second polka, or the next quadrille."

"Both. Cannot I have both? And take you to supper?"

"What a grasping man! Well, be it so."

"This is my dance, I believe, Mrs. Grey," put in a tall, light-haired youth with evidently 'dancing legs.'

Annie nodded assent, and went off with him.

Mr. Lascelles watched her from a distance, and Annie, seeing his fixed attention, smiled at him from time to time.

The quadrille followed, and she found her new acquaintance improving every moment.

"I must introduce you to some other lady," she remarked, during a short pause in their lively conversation, "if you stay the whole evening by my side, every woman in the room will declare that I keep you against your will, and every man will take up the quarrel to fight their own battle over the ladies' shoulders."

Mr. Lascelles yielded with the air of a martyr, and Annie chose out a pretty girl, very dull in speech, and a bright one, very plain in looks.

"Make your selection between these two," she said, indicating them by a wave of her jewelled fan, "they are the nicest women present."

"Oh!" said Mr. Lascelles, with a deep-drawn inspiration, "I cannot decide; I will be presented to both."

Mrs. Grey duly asked their permission, brought up Mr. Lascelles, presented him to Miss Amory and Miss Gardiner, saw him fairly launched in talk with the latter, and looking at the former, and then was

handed from partner to partner, as "Punch"
graphically describes a ballroom belle, "like a
pauper passed from parish to parish!"

At supper-time they comfortably established
themselves at a little table, and enjoyed the prospect
of a quarter of an hour's *tête-à-tête*, joined to a
truffled turkey, a partridge, strawberry-ice, and
champagne.

"Do you dislike to see women eat, Mr.
Lascelles?" said Annie, as she held out her plate for
a slice of partridge, "for if you do, I would advise
your giving up your seat and returning to Miss
Amory, whom I perceive yonder endeavoring to
make up her mind to insinuate that small
teaspoonful of water-ice between her cherry lips!"

"No, indeed; a graceful woman does every thing
gracefully. I am sure you would carve a goose and
then eat it quite as charmingly as you dance or
talk."

Annie bowed.

"Well, then, since my appetite will not throw you
into a syncope, what better time than the present,
while we sit so cosily in this corner, to tell me that
little secret?"

"What little secret?"

"When and where did you learn to admire me?"

Mr. Lascelles became suddenly grave.

"You know you promised that it should be told, if I would bring you here. My part is done, now yours!"

"Will you be very generous? Release me for this evening, and I faithfully, faithfully, Mrs. Grey, will tell you on the day of my departure!"

"Honor bright?"

"Yes."

"Very well. I will trust you. Give me some champagne, and now we must move, because those tender creatures have sipped their bird-like refreshment, and are on the wing!"

"I like this Englishman," thought Annie Grey, as she indolently unclasped her pearl bracelets in her bedroom that night, while Louise was brushing out her golden-tinged luxuriant hair, "he understands what I mean. And then he is something new— he is very nearly a sensation;" she yawned, stretched out her fair arms, "That will do, Louise. Good night."

The next morning Annie was languidly drinking her chocolate, and reading the "Herald" at twelve o'clock, when Mr. Lascelles and her brother Harry Newton were ushered in.

"Mr. Newton is answerable for my being here so

early," said Mr. Lascelles, as the lady gave him her hand; "he said that you would not refuse us."

"Harry was right. How d'ye do, Harry. Why were you not at the Lesters' last night?"

"Because I consider the 'Lesters' an undoubtful bore. I preferred playing billiards till eleven, and then I went to sleep in my own bed, instead of taking that repose in Mr. Lester's cloak-room for gentlemen."

"Pray tell me how you made Mr. Lascelles' acquaintance?"

"Mr. Somerton did me that honor an hour ago," replied Harry.

"You must not quite believe all that Harry tells you about this city," remarked Annie, turning to her visitor, "it is not a 'fast' place, for which mercy many good ladies are apt to turn up their eyes and say, 'Heaven be praised,' but it is a *very* respectable spot to live in. Harry has spent six years abroad; he considers it a great condescension when he comes back for a peep at us, and says shocking things about his dear compatriots. I grant you the society wants a little freshening up— a little burnishing. It needs improvement!"

"Improve a thing that does not exist! 'First catch your hare before you roast it,' is good counsel handed down from sage Mrs. Glasse, dear Annie. First form a society before you undertake to remodel it!"

"I noticed one thing last night," said Mr. Lascelles, "every lady whose name I asked—and as my conversation with Miss Amory was not very flowing, I frequently helped it on with questions about our neighbors—every lady was unmarried, with so few exceptions, that it struck me as being notable. There were no married ladies present, and I was told that married ladies never went out."

"Of course it would strike you. It strikes every stranger!" exclaimed Mr. Newton; "I have used my feeble efforts in vain. I have raised my weak voice till I was hoarse, striving to introduce a different order of things. I believe I could sooner fill a ballroom with dancing clergymen, than with young mammas who have married between seventeen and twenty, and who are entirely given up to the strictly private duties.'

"Are unions here happier than in other countries? Do the ladies find their reward for this sacrifice of all social pleasures in the consciousness of being more cherished, more loved, and more influential than anywhere else? Are their children better educated and better brought up? Are they better housekeepers? Do they make better puddings, pies, and shirts?"

"Don't be ironical Mr. Lascelles!" laughed Annie, setting down her cup, "and, moreover, it is not entirely the fault of the women themselves. Our society is destitute, *almost*, of married women for three reasons:

"First. Because the husbands don't care to go out, and won't willingly let their wives go without them.

"Secondly. Because their own inclination to do so is very small.

"Thirdly. For a reason which throws into the shade numbers one and two; because they are not invited!"

"Not invited!" exclaimed Mr. Lascelles.

"Not invited" repeated Mrs. Grey. "Who first began the system of reducing our society into the playful gambols of boys and girls, is not precisely known. Some people point to this or that family, and say, 'the so and so's first left out married sisters, even younger than the invited juvenile single ones;' but each person upon whom suspicion rests as the founder of this state of things, nervously rejects the honor; either names some one else, or carries back the date of the first such innovation to the dark ages —just after the Indians, I believe!"

"And does no one try to institute a reform?"

"Did you not hear Harry a moment ago? *He* preaches a new crusade. There stands the Peter who would carry the just war into every house, if he could ever find a trumpeter to sound the onslaught. But, be eloquent as he may, he makes no converts; that is, he finds a few who in words support him, but in action—" and Annie Grey's bright eyes and uplifted hands finished the sentence.

"Yes," said Mr. Newton, "I finally tried ironical praise. I handed about a little manuscript, purporting to be written to some newspaper, commending the bad taste of their proceedings. Some took it as the Princess Graciosa received the blows administered by her stepmother, wherein the rods turned into feathers when they touched the victim; my words were taken with calm composure, as being real praise due to a great reform. Others were indignant, and wondered 'what Mr. Newton could find to cavil at in our society;' but none agreed with me. I have rightly christened my humbled pages 'A Rejected Address.'"

"May I not see it?"

"If Annie has a copy, certainly."

Mrs. Grey searched among a pile of loose papers in her portfolio, and produced the following, which she read aloud, with comic earnestness:

"A REJECTED ADDRESS.

"Mr. Editor:—I have noticed for some time past, with unfeigned pleasure, a change which is stealing over our society. Will you allow me, through the medium of your valuable journal, to express to parents and guardians my just appreciation of their praiseworthy efforts. The honorable body of yourself and readers will easily understand that I allude to the prohibition of married persons, however young, at most parties of this gay season, or of any other. Every candid mind must acknowledge, that when once a young person is 'settled,' it should be for life; he or she should no longer haunt balls, as if still on preferment, but gracefully retire, leaving all standing room for those who *need* it. I believe it is a fact no longer to be doubted or disputed, that a young lady's first object is to marry—for this she is born, educated, and introduced—for this papa opens his purse-strings and doles out so many dollars per annum, to be devoted to dressing and party-giving. Now, is it to be borne with, that these same labors should be enjoyed by those who have no right to partake of them?

"If youthful matrons cannot comprehend all this, they must have it lucidly explained for them: if they will not give up society, they must be kicked out of it. It is the old story of the bees and the drones all over again.

"Imagine yourself, Mr. Editor, a bee or a beauty, toiling day by day to build your little cell for your private aggrandizement, and you find your honey, painfully extracted from flowers or flatterers, infringed upon by some worthless drone; who, with a home of her own, is still not content without dipping into your fund, and very often carrying off the larger portion. What would you do? Sting her out, of course, or die in the attempt!

"Such is the case with our ever-charming citizenesses; and success, I say, to their laudable undertaking. They only ask for fair play, and they ought to have it. 'We do not wish to exclude,' prattles some pretty pretender, 'any one, no matter how old, who is still on the look-out. They are all welcome; but when once suited, give way to the next batch.'

"Old-fashioned people, and people who have been abroad, have the impertinence to say that society formed on these principles is no society at all; but we all know that this is a humbug. Who cares for 'society' so called? Unmarried, young persons attend parties, and after that they should attend to their families. Were I called upon to get a wife, my choice would indubitably fall upon one of the present string of expectant damsels who, led out now for show, will, when chosen, joyfully practice what they preach, becoming good mothers of families and leave 'the world' to those who have occasion for its services.

"I trust the day is not far distant, when our saloons will no longer be (dis)graced by dancing Mrs., but around the walls a few elderlies in caps will keep 'watch and ward' upon their charges, while the floor will be occupied by those engaged in the true object of the dance, viz., marriageable persons of both sexes.

"In conclusion, I wish all manner of good wishes to the heads of families who agree with me, and who are sincerely engaged in this reform, and for those young ladies and gentlemen beginners, aiders, and abettors of this system, I earnestly pray that they will meet with a speedy fruition of their hopes. On comfort they *must* have—if they fail—it will not be their fault!

"I am, Mr. Editor, your humble

servant,

"A VETERAN."

"This has not helped to make you popular, I fancy, with every one," said Mr. Lascelles, laughing; "but of course the excluded married ladies are your friends!"

"Indeed, no," replied Mr. Newton; "I might be tempted to suppose that my impressions are wrong, and that my fair countrywomen are 'wedded to society;' for interference between them and it produces the result which attends all disinterested comings between husband and wife. The lovely victims are the first to attack one, and to wonder 'what I saw in their condition to excite my pity and remarks!'"

"Besides," interrupted Mrs. Grey, "of course this state of things pleases the multitude, or otherwise it could not exist. Unmarried sisters would resent the slight offered to married ones, and would not in their turn follow the example. Mothers would not tolerate such proceedings; but, indeed, nothing is more common than for a bride to invite none but girls to her wedding, thus signing cheerfully her own society death-warrant, while she signs her marriage settlement. She proceeds 'to fling wide

Hymen's banner,' and to rejoice that she is done forever with balls and parties and company, and can live happy and dowdy all the days of her young life."

The entrance of some visitors interrupted this discussion, and soon after Harry Newton and Mr. Lascelles took themselves off.

Pleasantly speeded the days of Charles Lascelles' stay. Harry Newton and himself were constantly together, and with her brother for chaperone Mrs. Grey went every where with impunity. The young Englishman was not anxious to extend his acquaintance. He found it very agreeable to saunter into Annie's drawing-room every morning, to chat merrily with her brother and herself, to dine with them, or to come back in the evening ready for a ball, if there was one; the opera, if it were opera night; the theatre, if any play or actor was worth the effort; or else to stay soberly at home, receive a few friends, or read aloud some new book. There was something which made Charles Lascelles grave, however. There was something weighing on his mind, which often rendered him silent and abstracted while the other two were jesting and talking.

At last the day was fixed for his departure.

"Do you know I leave on Thursday?" he said abruptly, one evening.

"Why do you go?" asked Harry.

"Because my father expects me. I promised to return on a certain day. Thursday is the very last moment that I can linger here."

"Do you remember your promise?" asked Mrs. Grey, looking up.

"Yes."

"Will you shirk it?"

"No."

"Then tell me now."

"Not till the time is fully elapsed. Stay, will you walk with me on Wednesday afternoon?"

Annie accepted, and they all talked about the approaching departure, and exchanged many vows of future friendship. Harry was to go abroad again in the summer. He promised to visit Mr. Lascelles at Dursley, his father's place in Bedfordshire.

On Wednesday, punctual to the appointed hour, Mr. Lascelles found Annie ready for her walk.

They went into one of the squares. It was early spring, and the trees were dismally bare still. She was impatient to hear the secret, which had been made important by its mystery.

"When and where did you learn to admire me?"

she asked for the third time with mock gravity.

"One day during last autumn," answered her companion, "I was idly walking down Broadway, when a charming face, bright with youth and animation, came out from a shop just beside me. The lady whose spirited countenance had attracted my decided attention was joined by another, older lady in black, and together the two proceeded in front of me. I was impertinent or curious or admiring enough to walk so closely upon them, that though I could not distinguish the words of their conversation, I could catch the fresh, vibrating tones of the younger lady, and occasionally her laugh would ring out upon my 'listening ear.' They went into Stewart's. I immediately wished for some gloves, and lingered as long as I could over the counter. I felt very much ashamed of my ungentlemanly conduct in pursuing, no matter how guardedly, a lady—no matter how worthy of pursuit —and returned to my hotel with a pair of brown eyes dancing before me.

"At the opera that evening, I was accompanied by a party of young men, who discussed the beauties in the house very freely. My abstracted air first amused and then annoyed them. They thought me dull company, and said so explicitly. I was parrying

their attacks, when suddenly a vacant box was filled
by three persons, and my spirits instantly rose.

"'Who can tell me,' I asked, 'the name of that
charming woman in peach-colored silk, with
drooping flowers in her hair?'

"Almost every lady wore a bonnet, so that this
one's costume was noticeable; it was so early in
November no *grandees* ensembles graced the opera;
but the object of my thoughts had evidently just
come from a dinner-party.

"My companions all raised their glasses, and as
we formed rather a conspicuous group, the
movement did not pass unperceived.

"The lady slightly blushed, drew her tulle scarf
closer around her white throat, and turned her back
upon us by the simple maneuver of giving her
whole attention to the gentleman who occupied the
chair behind her own.

"'You need not stare her out of sight,' I said,
rather pettishly, 'just let me know who she is?'

"No one could do that. Finally, I applied to Tom
Tremlet, known as 'Tattling Tom.' 'Stay!' said Tom,
'She is a stranger, I have seen her before though;
but then she was in deep mourning. She is a widow
I fancy; in fact I heard so then. It was a year ago,
and she passed like a flash through Saratoga. Her

name is Graves or Grey.'"

"It was I?" interrupted Annie, who had listened patiently, not *quite* understanding.

"Yourself!" replied Mr. Lascelles, "pray hear me out, and don't be tired. I could gather no further intelligence than this; and as the men bored me with their rallyings about my curiosity on the subject, I left them and stationed myself near you; but not where you could see me. How brilliant you were that evening, Mrs. Grey! I have often heard you talk well; I have often been charmed for hours by your wit and repartee, but never were you more agreeable than on that memorable occasion. The *entr'actes* were very long, I believe, and the lady with you was an old schoolmate, recently met; you were very happy, and your ideas, thoughts, and feelings flowed out with almost child-like delight. And yet, even then, I was more struck by a tone which promised a deeper depth in your mind than any you brought to light.

"I knew enough of you, I thought, while listening during those two hours, to convince me that you were the ideal every man forms for himself. I did not care to ask more about your belongings, I only wished to be introduced.

"When the opera was over, you got into one of

the carriages in waiting, and I heard the order given, 'Take Mrs. Grey home—New York Hotel.'

"They next morning—how early, I should be ashamed to confess—I commenced in earnest my interrogations. At last I found somebody that knew you.

"'Mrs. Grey of ——, you mean?' exclaimed Mrs. Taylor, the fluttering, flirting leader of the fashion; 'she is a very nice woman. Do you wish to know her? Unfortunately she left for Boston this morning.'

"Engagements detained me three days at New York. On the fourth I went to Boston. Twenty-four hours were spent in fruitless search there; at last I discovered that you had remained but two days, and were gone. No one knew where. I suppose I must have a very decided vein of eccentricity pervading my fabric, for here I was, a man of twenty-eight, running from city to city after a woman to whom I had never spoken, and whom I had seen twice.

"I returned to New York, bent upon bribing Mrs. Taylor to find out where you were resting in your travels, and to give me a letter of introduction to you. Alas! Mrs. Taylor had suddenly lost a sister, was in deep affliction, and received no one. You will scarcely believe that all this time I had never doubted your being a widow, had never asked the question, and in fact, as I will explain presently, saw an unshackled look about you which would almost by itself have led me to that opinion.

"After five weeks of hesitation, uncertainty, and wavering, I got credentials from some friends in New York, determined to break through the Lilliput ligatures of parties, dinners, and acquaintanceships, and came to this place. Mr. Somerton was the first person to whom I delivered a letter. After a short parley:

"'Do you know a Mrs. Grey?' I asked.

"'*The* Mrs. Grey, I suppose you mean,' replied Mr. Somerton, 'she is an intimate friend of my wife. And, by the way, instead of going alone to the Lesters' ball—for which I have got you a card— Mary had better carry you over to Mrs. Grey, and ask her to take you under her wing!'

"How joyfully I accepted, you may guess; how charmed I was, you doubtless saw; how miserably I felt when Mrs. Somerton told me, just after I left you, that there was a Mr. Grey. I hope you will never experience sufficient misery to understand.

"It was a great blow, and it seemed to me I deserved it all, because nothing could pardon my folly in blindly pursuing a woman of whom I knew nothing. At the very first I was inclined to find fault with you. I know I spoke with bitterness to Mrs. Somerton of your 'disengaged and unencumbered manners;' but afterwards I learned to excuse you. There was so much purity, so much propriety in your manner. You yourself were so unconscious of the effect of your style upon a stranger, that it would be unkind, unjust, to blame you seriously, because, a married woman, you had yet inspired a passion, stronger perhaps than any that gave their incense to your girlhood."

Mr. Lascelles spoke without one atom of vehemence or fervor. His words followed each other, as if it had been a lesson he was reciting; but Annie could not mistake their truth. He would not trust himself to utter his feelings except in this grave and strongly-controlled manner.

"Why do you tell me all this?" said Annie, gently "why not have gone away, leaving no secret between us, and letting me believe that our *friendship* was mutual, and no more?"

"Because I am going to venture a great liberty. I am going to assume a privilege which only your conviction of the deep I take in you, and your regret for the pangs you have unwittingly cost me, will forgive."

"What is it?" asked Annie, and she sat down upon a bench, weary and worried.

Mr. Lascelles seated himself beside her, and went straight on, without prelude and without hesitation, as he had spoken from the beginning.

"I told you that at first I blamed you, and was inclined to think harshly of you. I soon changed my mind. You are what strong circumstances and narrow prejudices in those around you have made you. You stand alone; you battle for your place in society. I never misjudged you after the conversation of that first morning visit. Your female companions, when you have any, are unmarried women, because the friends of your childhood are too busy, too absorbed to associate with any one out of their small domestic circle. Instead of the matronly dignity which would equally become your youthful charms, you have only the careless lightheartedness of a girl; and without quite understanding it, you encourage this heart-whole, fancy-free air. If you were for one instant to lapse into the thoughtfulness of the wife and mother, the tide would sweep over you, you would be washed quite out of sight, to that spot which I have heard elegantly assigned to all married women, 'the shelf.' You do not dislike your husband; but you know that it is through his mere existence that you are liable to be thrust aside, and you are consequently therefore, in danger of forgetting him altogether yourself, in trying to make others forget that he puts a barrier constantly between you and that gayeties you prize. Perhaps, if you had children, you would become just like your old schoolmates here, and never run the risk of breaking hearts. But I doubt it very much; you have been educated, your tastes are cultivated; *you* could not find your chief happiness in scolding servants and 'minding' children! You should live somewhere else. There is the great cure. You should live where your powers would be put to use. Where your thoughts would find an echo. Where a ball-room would not be your sole field, and dancing your sole enjoyment. Where you would see women of your own age, who have their own pursuits, and who *live*, not moulder!"

There was a pause.

"Do you forgive me, Mrs. Grey? Have I ventured too far?"

Annie held out her hand.

"I thank you," she said; "my manner does not need much improvement, and I will lay your counsel to heart. You give me more praise than is my due."

She rose, and they walked quietly home. It was a remarkable interview, and ended as calmly as it had begun.

"Did you have a pleasant walk?" asked Harry Newton, while they were taking tea.

"Very pleasant," both replied.

Mr. Grey was at home on this evening. He usually was at his club playing whist. Annie was wonderfully kind in her tone to him. So much so that the good man opened his eyes with surprise.

I would not answer for there not being a shade of malice in Annie's extraordinary tenderness. Mr. Lascelles had hinted at a coolness on her part to her husband, and perhaps she wanted to see if he enjoyed the sweet manner in which she addressed Mr. Grey, and inquired after his slight headache.

The next day, Harry Newton was with his friend, when the latter came to say good-bye.

"I did not wish to interfere with your sentimental leave-takings," said Harry laughingly to his sister, "but Lascelles brought me."

"Should you ever hear that I have forgotten you," were the Englishman's only whispered words, when Annie went to gather him a sprig of heliotrope from the box which filled her south window, "do not believe it. I may flirt, I may marry; but you have a place in my heart which never will own any other occupant. You are the romance of my life."

THE END.

THE WIDOW

CHAPTER I.

There was a stir upon the piazza of the United States Hotel at Saratoga. A half dozen of the finest beaux who, cigars in mouth, chairs balanced on two legs, and feet elevated on a line with their heads, were dreamily taking their afternoon smoke. They lazily arose one after the other and sauntered towards the objects that had aroused their indolent attention. Two horses, one a jet black, without a speck of white upon his shining coat, and the other a chestnut, both perfect specimens of horse beauty, stood pawing, and restlessly tossing their noble heads in front of the piazza steps, while a black groom in a livery of dark-green, held the reins as steadily and firmly in his hands as if he were an ebony statue placed there to accommodate equestrians.

"I don't know those horses Staunton, do you?" asked a youth, the down on whose upper lip, though darkened by a quantity of mustache wax, was just showing.

"No," replied Staunton, a gentleman of some eight and twenty years, taller by a full half head than his companions, and still more distinguished by his exceeding beauty of face and form. "They evidently belong to new comers. Look here, John, you who know everything and every body, whose mount is this?" turning to another of the group.

John Norton shook his head, but throwing away the end of his worn-out cigar, he leaned over the railing, and called to the silent servant in attendance. "I say, my friend, whose horses are those? Devilishly well groomed they are, and well they deserve it."

Thus appealed to, the man raised his head, respectfully touching his hat. "They belong to my mistress, sir," he replied, with imperturbabe gravity.

"Foiled, by Jove!" laughed Staunton; then taking from his waistcoats pocket a two-shilling piece, he tossed it to the discreet African, saying; "and what may 'my mistress' be named, my good fellow?"

The coin lay at the groom's feet, and he was stooping to raise it, when he suddenly resumed his attitude of perfect stillness, fixing his eyes intently upon the quivering ears of his charges, as if no mortal power could turn him from the contemplation.

The sweeping of a woman's skirt was heard upon the piazza, and the cluster of gentlemen fell back, with bows of excuse, to make way for a lady, a total stranger to all present. She was of a figure so justly and beautifully proportioned that the eye dwelt with pleasure upon its every curve. Scarcely reaching to the middle height, she held herself straight and erect with a jaunty air of her pretty head, that alone would have attracted attention. She wore a habit of dark gray cloth, turned back and trimmed with black, opening to the waist, and disclosing a shirt so beautifully embroidered, and fitting the bust so perfectly, that it spoke of Paris at a single glance. The hat was also gray, broad-brimmed, lined with black velvet, and ornamented with gray feathers, tipped with ebony. The riding gloves, a shade darker than the dress, showed off admirably a tiny hand. To relieve the sombre colors, a scarlet cravat of broad silk was tied beneath the chin, and a whip mounted in gold, and set around with large rubies, was fastened by a strong, short chain to her wrist, where it terminated in a plain bracelet, that was only discernible when it glittered through the opening of her gauntlet. The face corresponded to the lovely person. Not regularly handsome—not of those marble cut features that startle you at first by their perfect outline, but fail to satisfy a lifetime scrutiny —her's was a countenance delicious from its varied expression. The eyes were bright and wicked, with large, dark pupils, and light rims, now veiling themselves coquettishly beneath a real fringe of jetty lashes, then turning upon you with a glance of provoking archness. The lips were red, ripe, pouting, and the brow open, fair, and transparent. The hair of a sunny chestnut, arranged under a bandeaux, stopped its wavy descent sufficiently high upon the ear to show a pair of distracting hanging heart earring. Such was the outward appearance of the fair stranger, who rapidly glided through the throng of admiring gentlemen, acknowledging their salutation by a bend, like the easy swaying of a reed, her eyes cast down and her color rising.

The black horse was waiting for her, but turned

impatiently from side to side as the groom held out his open palm ready to aid his mistress.

"Ho, Selim, gently, sir, gently," said the lady, in a voice as sweet as ever sang, and before any of the gentlemen could eagerly offer their assistance, she had placed a delicate foot, with its boot of gray, upon the hand of her stable attendant, and with one light spring was in her saddle. Turning her bewildering eyes slowly and gravely upon Mr. Staunton, who had, as he hoped, happily been the nearest and quickest in his offer, "Thank you," she said in freezing tones. Then, dexterously smoothing the folds of her habit with one hand, while she restrained the curvetting of Selim with the other, she looked towards her groom. He was busily arranging the headstall of his own horse.

"What keeps you, Caesar?" she asked, while Selim danced up and down, and the firm little hand held the rein tightly. "Softly, Selim, softly."

"They have packed the wrong bit for Zelico, madam," answered Caesar, "he will never stand this severe one." A bound from Selim brought his rider to the side of Zelico. "Have you not another?" she asked, lowering her voice, and turning her back upon the staring group of men, whose numbers rapidly increased, and whose admiration for the

lovely equestrian grew while they watched her
superior horsewomanship.

"None of our own, madam," returned the servant.
"I will inquire at the stables."

"Hang Patrick's stupidity," said the vexed lady,
"for putting up the wrong bit, and you for not
discovering it sooner—go, Caesar."

"It would be a shame," said the unabashed Mr.
Staunton, who had followed close upon Selim's
heels, "it would be a shame to desecrate that noble
creature's mouth with vile livery-stable gear. I have
a bit, perfectly at your service, madam, if Caesar
will inquire for my servant, Mr. Staunton's servant,"
he continued, as if presenting himself, "and desire
him to hand it over."

When first addressed, the owner of the noble
Selim drew herself up, and haughtily gazed at the
intruder. At his name, her face relaxed, partially,
from its severity. The white lids drooped over the
brilliant eyes, then were slowly raised with a look,
which made Stanton's blood involuntarily rush
quicker through his veins, and a half smile slightly
played around the corners of her mouth.

"Thank you," she murmured again, but her tones
were this time more gracious; then recollecting the
bystanders, and perceiving a glance of intelligence

and a nod of freemasonry passing around the circle of Saratoga bloods, she impatiently, yet with much dignity, declined the proffered aid, and resuming her stately presence, put an end to the conference by hastily bowing, and galloping off, making a sign to Caesar to follow her on foot. Yet the enchantress in this single second found time to give another meaning, a soul-lit shot from beneath the edges of her eye-lashes, at this new victim of her charms. Staunton stood watching her amid the jeers and laughter of his companions. Reining up her horse, abruptly, when she was a stone's throw from the house, the lady resumed her colloquy with Caesar, which resulted in his return to the stables while she paced very leisurely along, patting the glossy sides of her beautiful Selim, and talking soft nonsense to him as if he were a child or a lover.

"Is she going to ride alone?" demanded John Norton. "If so, who'll escort her? Let's toss up. That slow gait seems to be an invitation. Charley won't answer—Charley's dead beat—eh, Charley?—she snubbed Charley!"

Charley Staunton joined in the laugh. "For all that, my friends, I'll bet a quarter box of cigars that I'll ride with her, with her own consent, before any of you do. And as for riding alone, no chance of that. There is Caesar scudding after her by the short cut, mounted on Zelico, after all. She sees him, and away she goes. By heaven, how she rides! Look at that trim figure. Isn't it a picture?"

"A gone case is our noble Charley," said one of the youths, "fallen prey to an unknown damsel or wife? Or what? Who knows? Let's ask Marvin. My opinion is—doubtful."

"It is rather singular for a lady to have such horses, and flourish such rubies, and no man to father them," sagely remarked Gerard Amyott, "and no look of 'family' about her. I'll bet she is a snob." Amyott's parents were thrifty biscuit bakers.

Appeal was made to Marvin. Who was the lady that owned two magnificent beasts and a groom in green livery? And had just gone to ride? When did she come? With whom did she come? Who did she know?

The replies, though ample, were not very satisfactory to curious people bent on elucidating mysteries. She came that day with her maid, and her man-servant, the groom. She brought a note from Judge——, commending her to the particular attention and services of Mr. Martin. She seemed to know no one; and her name was Mrs. Templeton Sydney.

"Mrs. Templeton Sydney!" "Whew." "Grand, but gingery that," was the amount of the valuable remarks made by the sapient gentlemen, who thus picked our heroine to pieces.

"Have you heard the news, Miss Latimer?" asked Gerard Amyott, of a fair girl, one of a group of ladies, now filling the piazza, ready for their afternoon rides and drives.

"What news?" said Emily Latimer, and "What news?" echoed four or five voices. Why, Charley Staunton has fallen head over ears in love with a will-o'-the-wisp lady on horseback, who rode away just now, carrying his heart at her saddle bag."

"But won't she come back and bring the heart?" demanded a lady in a sharp, quick tone, with eyes as sharp as her voice, "because, if she does not, we lose Mr. Staunton entirely, everybody being aware that Mr. Staunton is 'all heart'".

"A thousand thanks, Miss Thornley, for your valuable opinion—I prize it—but did none of you from your lattice windows, see this fair possessor of myself?"

"I did," said Emily Latimer, "is she handsome? Her dress was not. The ugliest color I ever saw, and badly fitting, and her shirt was horridly embroidered. I didn't look at her face, but she seemed common."

"Bravo," said Charley Staunton, "are you engaged for the cotillon this evening, Miss Emily?"

"No," said Emily, eagerly.

"I am," drawled Charley. "Let me hand you to the carriage." And the party drove off.

CHAPTER II.

It was "ball" night at the United States Hotel, which means a full room, fine music, beautiful dancing, and handsome women—sometimes. The evening was half over, and Charley Staunton still strolled about. Not the entreating looks of Annie Montgomery, nor the winning smiles of Mrs. Beresford, not the openly expressed wish of Edith Amyott (an old favorite), nor the pleading eyes of Emily Latimer, not even the perfect dancing of Cynthia Sherwood, could induce the "best dancer" to attempt one step on this memorable night. He made his way into every coterie—he scanned every crowd of gossiping women, but all in vain—he peeped into every corner of the piazza—no sign of the fair equestrian. Had she, indeed, prolonged her ride till midnight? Or was she sulking in her own apartment? That last doubt was easily solved. To fly to the bar, to find the number of Mrs. Sydney's room, to creep along the corridors and joyfully perceive no gleam of light from the lady's chamber, this was the work of five minutes, and Charley then resumed his search. "That she is a lady, I am sure," he muttered half aloud, as he was slowly proceeding through a shady part of the piazza. A figure moved, hitherto concealed in the darkness—a white arm emerged from a mass of drapery, and gleamed in the pale moonlight; a lady was rising from the sofa and drawing her shawl closer around her as she did so. With a crash, a heavy bracelet fell to the ground. How Staunton rejoiced! In a moment he had recognized his enslaver, and secured the jewel.

"Permit me," said he, "to introduce myself to Mrs. Sydney. She is a stranger here, and there is no one to perform the ceremony for me. There are some cases where formality must be banished. Am I excused?"

"Your pertinacity is worthy of a better cause," said Mrs. Sydney, laughing. "I must, I suppose, pardon a presumption brought out by the force of my charms, is not that it? Your name is not unknown to me, Mr. Staunton, but ask no questions as how it has reached me."

"I care not to ask," gallantly replied the gentleman. "It is sufficient happiness to learn that I have already been mentioned in your presence. If for evil, I trust to do away with the impression, if for good, then so much the better. But won't you kindly, as I am no stranger, make room for me on that sofa? Though you would not accept my offer of 'bit, bridle, and bridoon,' I am now so little embarrassed, and feel so brave, that I demand an even greater favor: let me clasp your bracelet?"

"Willingly," replied Mrs. Sydney, "for either I must try your skill, or else call upon the services of my waiting damsel. The mechanism of that clasp defies the solitary power of one hand only. You must take me to the light, however."

Indifferently she took his arm, and they walked to a lamp in the passageway, by the aid of whose brilliancy Mr. Staunton undertook to fasten three separate chains, each of which was connected by a curious locket. How they all three came undone together was a perfect surprise! The bare, round arm of Mrs. Sydney, as cold as marble, and as soft as velvet, patiently kept its extended position, while Mr. Staunton leisurely proceeded with his pleasant task. It is no disagreeable thing to be thus employed, with one's eyes more bent upon the curved wrist than upon the bracelet, each link studded with a huge gem, and the same stones forming a rose and bud in the center with leaves of green enamel. The pleasantest things always end the soonest, however, and Mr. Staunton found he must finish his task, because the beautiful arm began to move impatiently, and the fair owner spoke:

"Are you awkward? Or dull? Or what, Mr. Staunton? Julie never took half so long in her whole service of five years."

"There, it is done, and very cleverly executed, I think," replied Mr. Staunton, looking at his work admiringly. "But why are you sitting in the piazza, Mrs. Sydney? Are balls charmless for you? Does dancing offer no inducements to face an admiring crowd? Let me persuade you. I have been teased the whole evening to dance; with you as a partner, I will retract all former refusals."

"Thanks. For dancing, I have a very decided fancy, and feel really inclined to accept your daring offer—daring, because, how do you know but that I dance outrageously? And then my dress. This large shawl may cover a multitude of defects, which would shine glaringly in the ball-room, and might shock Miss Latimer & Co."

"I will stand the shock in both instances."

"Will you take me in the Yankee phrase, 'sight unseen,' or shall I favor you beforehand?"

She carelessly dropped her shawl, and displayed a perfect wardrobe, so fresh, so unsullied: her dress of a light white texture, trimmed with a wealth of lace, and a bodice of emeralds that a duchess might have envied. The figure amply redeemed the promise made in the riding-habit. Staunton was dazzled. He bowed low, but a triumphant light was in his eye, as he thought how he had outwitted the rest, and of the sensation he would presently create. Did Mrs. Sydney divine the thought? There was a mirthful archness in her brilliant eyes, and the little scarlet lip quivered with amusement.

Very lovely she certainly was, and as they entered the ballroom, their success was quite astonishing. The German cotillion was on the point of being formed, and Staunton led his prize to a seat in the ring. The ladies looked shy, she was so pretty and so graceful. Truth to say, they never would have been half so worried for her character had she been ten years older, and slightly pock-marked. But the whisper ran around—"She brought a letter from Judge ——, and then—see her jewels—she must be very rich." So calumny dropped her voice, and only sneered behind her fan.

The cotillon was led by James Roberts, of course. Dear little James! Blessings on your curled mustache, so carefully bedewed with bandoline. And those tender arms always moving in cadence to the music. This may, perchance, never meet your eyes; but accept a little tribute from an admiring stranger. You are, indeed, the prince of "leaders." Had Vestris lived to see your day, even he might have allowed his mantle as *"Dieu de la danse,"* to fall upon your delicate shoulders. There is none quite like you, only you have a sharp way of keeping time on your partner's knees. Change that, dear James, and your dance is superhuman.

Now, though Charley Staunton had boldly undertaken to possibly compromise himself with an unknown danseuse, still an inward tremor made him eager for, and yet afraid of, the first "turn." Suppose, in spite of her exquisite figure, she should be "heavy in hand," he thought. In a few minutes the leader took out Mrs. Sydney, and his partner, Cynthia Sherwood, did the same by Staunton. Charley maneuvered till he stood opposite his prize.

The figure was danced, and away they whirled.

"All right," thought Mr. Staunton, exultingly. Mrs. Sydney danced as she rode, perfectly. Polka, waltz, and schottische were equally fields in which she displayed her talent.

Cynthia Sherwood was angry; none of the ladies exactly liked it; but the men—oh! They were subdued.

It was an evening of triumph. Many women would have flushed and showed their exultation. Not so Mrs. Templeton Sydney. Not a warmer tint dyed her cheek; not a strand of her smooth hair was discomposed; and a saucy light in the gray eye alike welcomed every compliment.

"At what hour do you breakfast?" asked Mr. Staunton, when, the ball over, he took leave at the foot of the staircase.

"At ten, or thereabouts. Good night. Julie, the lights," and Mrs. Sydney vanished.

CHAPTER III.

"Not a trace of fatigue on cheek or brow, Mrs. Sydney," said Mr. Staunton, as that fair lady took her seat at the breakfast table, and he joined her. "I see no duplicate in you of the jaded looks opposite and beside us."

"No compliments at someone else's expense," said Mrs. Sydney. "I think these ladies look very bright. Just see Mrs. Hartman and Miss Power, surely they exhibit no unusual paleness."

Charley Staunton laughed. "You know every thing at once. Anyone would suppose that you had assisted those two ladies in choosing their rouge.

But what will you have for breakfast? The usual course? Eggs, omelette, chops, toast, chicken, coffee, and rolls—will that do?"

"About enough, I think. But I place myself this morning in your hands—order my breakfast, and I'll eat it, if possible."

While Mr. Staunton's waiter was rushing in search of the desired articles, Mrs. Sydney raised her eye-glass to take a look at her surroundings, and her companion looked at her.

"You will not see *'le choix du choix'* at this table," he said. "*We* breakfast and dine in private rooms at the restaurant, hours after this time. I rose early this morning, and breakfast here solely in your honor." Mrs. Sydney did not appear overcome by the compliment.

"Ah," she replied, negligently, "most of the fashionables live in cottages too, do they not?"

"The Redwoods do, and the Elwyns, and a good many others. Are you acquainted with them, may I ask?"

Mrs. Sydney turned her eyes for a second towards the questioner. "No," she quietly answered.

Here the eggs, omelets, and chops began to arrive in battalions, and the business of eating commenced. Meanwhile, the score or two of ever-changing breakfasters watched with the most eager scrutiny the simply dressed, but yet most marked-looking woman, whose beauty and emeralds had drawn all eyes the night before. Mr. Staunton's attentions were already voted 'very strange.'

"Pray, give me some more of that chicken," said Mrs Sydney, and "make no outcry at my appetite."

"You are a New Yorker, I perceive," said Charley, as he helped her, "not afraid of being plump, and starving yourself accordingly, as too many women from there do." This was only a chance shot of Master Charley's, who sided thus delicately to find out whence came the fair stranger. "No," was again the unsatisfactory and short reply. "Will you be long at Saratoga, Mrs. Sydney? A stupid, commonplace question, but one of great interest to me."

"It depends upon how I like it. I am very new at watering-place life, old as I am. What horrid coffee!"

"Try tea. Joseph, some tea. 'New at watering-places,' did you say? Why, where on earth, then, do you pass your summers?"

"At my own country-seat, or at my brother's," quietly responded the provoking Mrs. Sydney. "Who is that pretty girl just entering the room?" she continued; "what a pity that these women should destroy the desired effect of full-dress by exhibiting bare arms and stripe shoulders in the morning."

"I notice that you do not follow their example," said Mr. Staunton, "and I must agree with you, that those flowing draperies of muslin and lace which partially conceal your arms, are more suitable to the 'garish light of day.' But custom appears to have decided, that at Saratoga, from morning till morning, the ladies must never relax from the extremity of a severe grand appearance. The gentlemen, more privileged, indulge in white coats and loosely tied neckcloths, unreproved."

"Poor women!" said Mrs. Sydney, compassionately. She rose from the table, and carelessly shook off some crumbs from her exquisitely white morning-dress.

The old worn-out simile of a swan upon a lake involuntarily occurred to Mr. Staunton. As he followed her, she swept so nonchalantly along. The train of her dress, with its multitude of fluted frills, gave dignity to her slight figure; with her chestnut hair simply arranged, she looked so fresh, so unlike the exposed beauties who were beginning their daily and eternal promenades in the piazza.

"Will you go to the bowling alley, Mrs. Sydney?"

"Definitively then, you take me under you care,

Mr. Staunton? Are you a free man, and can safely venture?" asked Mrs. Sydney, smiling.

"Venture? As how?"

"No one to be made jealous?"

"And after? What is that to me?"

"Oh, you are very kind. Pray, add to your favors by catching a waiter, and dispatching him for my maid. Or stay, I will go myself. I wish my garden hat, and Caesar will come for his orders for the day. Smoke your morning cigar, and then you will find me in the drawing room. *Au revoir*."

The piazza gradually filled. Charley Staunton smoked his cigar and beat time upon the railing with his dandified little stick. He exchanged nods with some tired-looking fast men just crawling out for their day's diversion, and raised his hat indolently to some distant groups of promenading ladies.

"How's the conquest?" asked Gerard Amyott, seating himself beside our hero, and signifying his wish for a light by extending his hand to Charley's cigar.

"What conquest?" demanded Charley.

"The Templeton Sydney. All right, eh?'

"You be d—d," replied Charley Staunton.

"Amyott,—once for all—you do not know Mrs.

Sydney. Oblige me by letting her name drop," and Mr. Staunton walked off to peer through the drawing room windows. His search was successful: away went the cigar; he disappeared, reappeared and brought out on his arm the late subject of remark.

The fair Saratoga belles fought very shy of Mrs. Templeton Sydney, but the men gathered around Mr. Staunton and his charge. Those who had danced with her the night before came up to renew their acquaintance, and many others solicited an introduction. Then they were disappointed. This supposed lioness, this unprotected young woman was so cool, so calm, so unbending beyond a certain point; there was such a satirical light in her saucy eyes, and so much to match upon her tongue, that after a hard rap or two, the boldest of the polite assaulters began to hang fire. How Charley Staunton enjoyed it. Mrs. Sydney knocked down the tenpins, necessarily, with as much grace and ease as she floored the men. There was no fuss, no parade. Her model of a hand clasped the ball with apparently a delicate touch. She sent it along carelessly, and softly it did its work of destruction. Such plaudits followed her third successive spare, that the alley on which she was playing now became the center of attraction. Certainly, she was very pretty. A soft rose color bloomed upon her cheek, and yet she looked so deliciously unconscious of the homage paid to her charms. A French marquis was presented; she spoke like a *Parisienne* born. Then a Spaniard; and her fluent address quite transported him. Finally, a German, just caught, a grave doctor of law, made her a bow, while glancing up through his eyebrows. Mrs. Sydney answered with a smile brighter than sunbeams, and with an accent which declared her mistress of the language. This was too much. Everybody left the alley. Who would stay with such a bold, outrageous, unknown woman?

Charley Staunton grew desperate. If love at first sight never before had a victim, he was a candidate.

"When do the cars arrive?" asked Mrs. Sydney.

"Presently."

"Suppose we witness the disembarkation?"

"Most willingly," agreed Charley Staunton. Mrs. Sydney made the move. She drew on her glove, and followed by a covey of beaux, made her way back to the house.

"There is to be a party to the Lake, tomorrow," said John Norton. "Mrs. Elwyn gets it up. Are not you going, Mrs. Sydney?"

"I don't know Mrs. Elwyn."

"But any other lady of the party can invite you?"

"I don't know any lady at Saratoga," again replied Mrs. Sydney.

The men exchanged looks. Charley Staunton bit his lip.

Cynthia Sherwood, Annie Montgomery, a lively Mrs. Scott Morris, and two of the Elwyn girls stood waiting in the piazza for stray men to go to walk, or to dance, or to do any thing. On the approach of Mrs. Sydney, they bridled up and sailed away in the opposite direction.

Mrs. Sydney drew down the corners of her arch lips and looked amused.

"Here come the new arrivals," said Mr. Norton, "and heading the list is Harry Stuart, I vow."

"Mr. Stuart?" echoed the flying damsels, returning with eager looks.

A handsome young man, evidently a Southerner, sprang from the car. A dozen hands were extended to meet him, "How d'ye do?" "How are you?" "Glad to see you."

"Come at last, Mr. Stuart?" said Mrs. Morris, with an overwhelming smile. There was a perfect chorus of rejoicings. Certainly, this must be a very popular and immensely rich individual.

Mr. Stuart returned the greetings with friendly warmth, but his eye glanced around impatiently. In a moment he had spied Mrs. Sydney.

"My dear, imprudent Rose," he exclaimed, seizing her around the waist, "how have you got on without me?"

Charley Staunton looked furious. The rest of the party was amazed.

"Ah, Staunton," he continued, "you recollect Rosa, I see. It must be fully sixteen years since you saw her."

"My dear fella," said Mr. Staunton, "I am perfectly puzzled. I never saw Mrs. Sydney before. What is she to you?"

"Why, my sister, Charley! You saw her as a little, wee girl, ages ago, at the South, when your mother brought you there for your health. Have you been playing mysterious, Rosa?"

"Rather so," said Mrs. Sydney, smiling. "But Mr. Staunton and I are very good friends, though we did not renew our childish romps."

"I am glad to hear it. Miss Cynthia, what are you all after here? Is Saratoga exciting? Dear Mrs. Morris, you are brighter and fresher than ever. How do you kill the time?"

"Oh, pretty well," replied Mrs. Morris, "though I

must confess, that the snake is scotched, not killed. Your arrival will quite annihilate the enemy;" then, in a half-whisper, "Pray present me to your lovely sister." The rest of the ladies made the same request.

"Rosa, dear," said Mr. Stuart, "Mrs. Scott Morris, Miss Sherwood," Mrs. Sydney curtsied low, with the most provoking air of deep respect, and, as her eyes during the greeting were of course cast down, Mrs. Morris was free to suppose that this was the reason why her proffered hand remained unshaken.

"Suppose, Harry," said Mrs. Sydney, when she had executed this obeisance, without listening to one of the flattering words that Mrs. Morris was showering upon her, "suppose you see after your room. Though secured days ago, some individual, hungry for rest and comfort, may pop into it."

"Good advice, my child. And I have a letter in one of my trunks for you from—

"Good heaven, Harry, what is that cut on your cheek? Come here." Rosa carried him off to a corner of the piazza, where she whispered a few words. He nodded, laughed, and they walked into the house together.

"So the fair Mrs. Sydney is Stuart's sister; and you, ladies, have been rather too quick in sending her to Coventry?" said John Norton, laughing wickedly.

"How will your friend Mr. Stuart like your treatment of his precious 'Rosa,' Miss Elwyn? Your mamma said you would not have her to the Lake party tomorrow at any price."

Miss Elwyn had long been suspected of making yearly summer sieges to Mr. Harry Stuart's heart, and though the agreeable Southerner had never decided, neither had he ever rejected the Elwyn's attention, so that Miss Emily Elwyn still "dwelt in a land of hope."

"Of course we shall ask Mrs. Sydney. I will go to mamma at once," replied the young lady, taking possession of Mr. Amyott's arm, which hung unoccupied by his side. Mr. Amyott was not surprised. Free and easy manners have long been "the go" with a certain high set.

The group separated, and Charley Staunton, who was unusually quiet and silent, paced up and down the piazza. Anyone who had had the liberty of inquiring into his thoughts would have found them to run something like this: "So my fair widow is my friend Stuart's sister. She is the little Rosa Stuart that I met at her father's plantation when she was a pretty chicken of some six years, and I a shy, delicate boy of eleven, and rather afraid of Harry's boisterous games. This accounts for her knowledge of me—but why did she keep it secret? By heaven, what an empress-like air she looked at those women after her mock courtesy! She is such a beauty! 'Charley Staunton in love?' 'Never!' But by Jove, I'm afraid 'tis true. What grace—what esprit— what"… But we need not follow the gentleman's mental rhapsodies any further.

CHAPTER IV.

The reader may fancy all the politeness with which Mrs. Templeton Sydney was now overwhelmed by the elite of Saratoga.

Mr. Stuart's reputation for wealth, and his personal popularity, made him an object of excessive interest wherever he appeared. To neglect or snub his sister was an idea not to be endured by anyone. It was singular and amusing to watch the attentions that were now showered upon the once doubtful lady. Mrs. Elwyn came in person to insist upon Mrs. Sydney's presence at the Lake party. After much difficulty, Rosa consented—only yielding at last to her brother's request.

The party went off with great success. Mrs. Sydney wore a pink dress of a new and surprising shade, and sang extraordinarily beautiful Indian airs, which ravished the company, and put the final stroke to her numerous conquests. And then, she was co-heiress with her brother, people said.

The next day, Rosa, from a whim, kept her room, but promised to ride with Mr. Staunton in the afternoon. Behold them, therefore, mounted; Charley triumphantly whispered to Gerald Amyott, "Aren't you glad you did not take up that wager, my fine fellow? You would have been 'done,' I think."

"Do you ride or drive, Harry?" asked Rosa, as she took her whip from her brother.

"Neither," he answered. "I have a friend to meet, whom I expect presently. Be off with you." He gave his sister a merry nod. She snapped the clasp of her bracelet, looked up, gave him a saucy smile with her finger to her lip, and then dashed off.

"Which way shall we go, Mr. Staunton? You may choose."

"Very well; trust to my taste, and you will not repent it. I know a 'bosky dell' and a nice greensward for a canter. This way. How well you ride, Mrs. Sydney."

"I deserve no great credit for it," answered the lady. "I was put on horseback as soon as I could sit straight in a chair, and Harry took immense pains with me. Besides, I was thoroughly taught in England, and even in Hyde Park gained some applause for my equestrian performances."

"Which do you prefer as a country to live in, England or France?"

"I shall answer like a child between the rival merits of cake and candy—both. Just at present I choose England. At least, I suppose I do," and she laughted and looked mischievous.

"Why?" said Mr. Staunton.

"Simply because I am going there. I am too wise not to reconcile myself to circumstances. I sail in the Baltic, on the 16th."

"Good heaven!" exclaimed Charley—"so soon— then you leave Saratoga shortly?"

"Prepare yourself for the sad event. I may sadly announce this as being, in theatrical parlance, my last night but one."

Mr. Staunton's face expressed the deepest disappointment. "Is this true?" he inquired, with a voice really tremulous. The dandy had totally disappeared—he was only a man desperately in love. "Dear Mrs. Sydney, are you jesting? Believe me, your movements have an entire control over mine. I may be hasty. You may think me impertinent to dare on so short an acquaintance to make such a declaration—but wherever you go, I must follow. Pardon my rashness. Do not answer me now," as he saw her about to speak. "Give me time to prove my devotion. Permit me the opportunity to prove how —"

"I *must* speak, Mr. Staunton," said Mrs. Sydney, impetuously interrupting him. "This has gone too far. Forget what you have just said. I shall only remember it as proof of flattering friendship. Without another word, listen to a little anecdote, which must be my only excuse for what you will do almost right in calling my heartless coquetry." There was an earnest look of regret in Mrs. Sydney's beautiful eyes. Mr. Staunton bowed, and was somewhat stunned. It was his first offer of love. An awkward business for a novice, anyway, but rendered doubly so by the mysterious manner in which his declaration was received.

"Do you remember," said Mrs. Sydney, "the grand fancy ball given by Mrs. Francourt the winter after her return from France, years ago? It was to be a surprising affair, and we arrived, my father and myself, in New York, a day or two before it was

given. We were on our way to Europe, partly for my
health, partly for my education. I was a thin, sallow,
sickly girl of fifteen, just recovering from a long
illness, during which I had lost my hair, and my
head was covered, not adorned, with a cap. I heard
of this ball at the hotel where we lodged, and was
seized with a girlish desire to be present.

I had only one acquaintance in New York, Miss
Walton. Miss Walton asked us to dine with her.
Papa was very much occupied, and I went alone.
There were two other guests, a gentleman and a
lady—both young. The lady was a cousin, it
seemed, of the gentleman, very pretty, very
beautifully dressed, and forming, I must confess,
with her friend, the lovely Miss Walton, a great
contrast to poor little me. I was all bundled up in a
bright shot silk of every color, and made to show off
a style still sacred and cherished among the
dressmakers of my native city. Then, my cap was
too late, and old enough for my grandmother. It fell
over my eyes, and increased my awkwardness by
necessitating a continued hitching up to clear my
sight. Miss Walton was very kind to me, and so was
the charming Mrs.—" Rosa paused, smiled,
switched the leaves from a neighboring tree, and
added, "Mrs. Dudley." Mr. Staunton started. He

began to understand.

"I did not catch the gentleman's name when he was presented to me, but during the course of the dinner I heard it. I had been introduced as 'Miss Stuart, from the South,' a common name, which seemed to make no more agreeable impression upon the gentleman than my appearance had done. He took so little notice of me, that though I had a right to claim his attention on discovering who he was," Rosa glanced at her companion, "I never dreamed of doing such a thing. He appeared wrapped up in his pretty cousin. She hectored and coaxed him, and scolded and cajoled him by turns, as I sat amazed at her varied humors.

"Dinner over, we were soon joined by our only cavalier, Mr. Walton having betaken himself to his club. Mrs. Walton was an invalid; and as she seldom left her chamber, Mary took me up stairs to see her. On our return, a servant stopped Miss Walton to give her a message. She begged me to go on to the drawing room, and though I was dreadfully afraid of encountering the lively couple there without Mary's guardian presence, still I was forced to proceed. On entering the smaller room, which was dimly lighted, I caught the sound of my name, pronounced with a laugh. Mrs. Dudley was lying back in a huge chair, protecting her face from the blazing fire with her fan, and smiling up brightly into her cousins eyes as he leant over her.

"'We can't help ourselves,' said the little lady. 'Mary is bent upon our taking her. Being in mourning, she can't go, so that we are to be sacrificed. Don't look so doleful, child. You must dance with her, of course; but to save sneers, I'll tell everybody what an heiress she is. She is not so very ugly. She has nice eyes, and little hands, though they are so brown.'

"For my life, I could not have moved. I stood silent, mortified, spell-bound. 'I should not mind her uglyness,' answered the gentleman, 'if she were not so ungainly and stupid. While you and Miss Walton were chatting away at dinner, there she sat like an mute, nothing to say, and not pretty to look at. She is a great mistake from beginning to end, from her cap to her ill-made slippers."

"'Wait, *mon cher,* till she comes home from Paris. I'll live to see you in love with her yet. She is *so* rich,' and Mrs. Dudley laughed.

"'In love with such a girl! Not if she were John Jacob Astor's only child! My sweet Clara, I have a different standard.'

"Mary Walton's step was heard in the

passageway; I flew to meet her. 'I could not go in, my dear Mary,' said I. 'I am too foolishly timid among strangers. Don't tell on me, though.' Mary promised.

"They talked of the ball when we joined them. Mrs. Dudley offered to chaperone me, but my fancy was passed. I awkwardly thanked her, and declined as firmly as my stammering lips could form the words. Her cousin looked vastly relieved. In a few days we sailed for Europe. There I spent six years. There I was married, and returned soon after to America with my husband, to whom I had been betrothed from my infancy. Mr. Sydney lived but a year. Since his death, I have never left the South, till now. That is why you heard me say I knew nothing of watering-places in this country. I wished, before leaving America again, to get some insight into the life at such resorts. Saratoga was chosen as the best field. Just as we were quitting New York, three days ago, my brother received a letter which postponed his departure from that city. I was all packed, ready to start, and unwilling to delay. I overcame his objections to my traveling alone with my servants, and reached here in safety. On coming down to mount my horse that afternoon, you recollect the stares of the crowd, and your offers. At first, I did not look at or remember you. But on your mentioning you name, a sudden spirit of mischief seized me. Yes, the gentleman so eager to place his bridle and his services at my feet was the disdainful cousin of pretty Mrs. Dudley, my old playfellow on the banks of the Savannah. He had a second time failed to recognize me. Involuntarily rushed through my mind, 'In love with such a girl! No! Not if she were John Jacob Astor's only child!' and I vowed a woman's vow, that you should be in love with 'such a girl.' Can you forgive my unkind vanity? I never suspected that you would go so far. I have learned to like you so much during the past three days, that I would gladly spare you any pain. As I said before, forget your words to me just now, or only let them be considered as a renewal of our childish intimacy." She held out her hand. Mr. Staunton took it and pressed it warmly.

"Of course, I soon recognized my silly self in your story, dear Mrs. Sydney, and I am ready to curse my presumptuous folly. But, is it because I did not admire you at fifteen, and had the careless impertinence to let you hear it, that you now scorn my suit? I will delightedly forgive your revengeful designs upon me, if you will overlook my coxcombry, and not shake your head in that decided manner."

"There was another reason," said Mrs. Sydney, blushing and turning away, "pray do not continue this subject. Let us take a canter now, and then we must turn our horses' steps homewards."

Rosa began to talk in her usual charming manner. She forced her distracted companion to listen to her, at least, if he would not follow her topics.

She spoke of Italy, of Switzerland, of Paris, of London. Scenery and society she discussed with equal spirit and truth. Now playful, then caustic, she praised fully with a single sentence, or condemned with a trenchant word. The ride was over. As they drew rein at the piazza steps, Harry Stuart came out to meet them. "He is come," he whispered to his sister. A gentleman with a strikingly high-bred English air hastily followed Mr. Stuart. Though with true English reserve he strove to hide his emotion, he colored violently as he took Mrs. Sydney's hand, and his bright blue eyes were fixed with uncontrollable admiration upon her. Rosa gathered up her riding-skirt, and left the little hand a moment longer than etiquette requires in that of the stranger. Charley Staunton was jealous, annoyed, inquisitive. "Permit me to present two of my friends to each other," said Mrs. Sydney with a graceful embarrassment, as new to her as it was becoming. "Mr. Staunton, Mr. Montague."

"Change your dress, my dear Rosa," said Mr. Stuart, "we are just going to tea."

Mrs. Sydney nodded, and Mr. Montague followed her down the corridor, and stood talking at the foot of the stair, while she listened with a pleased expression and drooping eyelids.

"Handsome fellow, isn't he?" said the unconscious Harry, "and so clever, and so attached to Rosa. He is second son to Lord ——, but has a good fortune through his mother. It is an admirable match, and they will make a devilishly handsome couple. They first met abroad."

So that was the end of Charley Staunton's first real love affair. He almost groaned. For, though a dandy, Charley had a heart.

"They are engaged, then?" he managed to bring out, directing his glass across the lawn to one of the cottage.

"Oh, yes! They have been engaged for three months. Lawyers are so slow. And then, to spare Montague the fuss of one of our public weddings, which Rosa hates too, they are to be married quietly next week in New York, and sail on the 16th. His people are dying to see her. But this is a secret.

Don't put it about here. Anyway, Montague will be sufficiently stared at. 'A rag of quality,' as Horace Walpole calls himself, is so taking with our countrymen."

No danger of Charley Staunton putting about Mrs. Sydney's engagement. On her reappearance, she guessed that Harry had told the secret, and she looked kindly and with a sort of sisterly affection at her rejected admirer.

The hours passed swiftly. The party left Saratoga. Harry invited Mr. Staunton to the wedding.

He went, and congratulated the bridegroom, and on parting, begged the beautiful bride to wear an offered token occasionally.

It was a costly ring, which bore three dates: his visit to the South; the evening of Miss Walton's dinner; and the ride at Saratoga.

ABOUT THE AUTHOR

Susan Petigru King-Bowen was born on October 24, 1824 in Charleston, South Carolina. She was educated at Madame Talvande's School for Young Ladies in Charleston and later at Madame Guillon's boarding school in Philadelphia.

After her father suffered deep financial losses in the Panic of 1837, King's mother urged her to marry for money. The resulting marriage to Henry C. King was a rocky one that influenced much of her later writing on love and marriage.

Her first novel, *Busy Moments of an Idle Woman*, was published anonymously in 1853. She continued to author books and write stories for publications like *Harper's Magazine, Russell's Magazine* and the *Charleston Daily Courier* for the next two decades.